MORAL, BELIEVING ANIMALS

MORAL, BELIEVING ANIMALS

HUMAN PERSONHOOD AND CULTURE

CHRISTIAN SMITH

OXFORD

UNIVERSITY PRESS

2003

OXFORD
UNIVERSITY PRESS

Oxford   New York
Auckland   Bangkok   Buenos Aires   Cape Town   Chennai
Dar es Salaam   Delhi   Hong Kong   Istanbul   Karachi   Kolkata
Kuala Lumpur   Madrid   Melbourne   Mexico City   Mumbai   Nairobi
São Paulo   Shanghai   Taipei   Tokyo   Toronto

Copyright © 2003 by Oxford University Press, Inc.

Published by Oxford University Press, Inc.
198 Madison Avenue, New York, New York 10016

www.oup.com

Library of Congress Cataloging-in-Publication Data
Smith, Christian (Christian Stephen), 1960–
Moral, believing animals : human personhood and culture /
Christian Smith.
p. cm.
Includes bibliographical references.
ISBN 0-19-516202-1
1. Philosophical anthropology.   2. Sociology—Philosophy.   I. Title.
BD450 .S555 2003
301—dc21   2002154507

1   3   5   7   9   8   6   4   2

Printed in the United States of America
on acid-free paper

ACKNOWLEDGMENTS

I owe a debt of gratitude to many people who have had some hand in bringing this book to fruition. Many scholars and friends read earlier drafts of chapters and provided very helpful criticisms and encouragements, including Roger Lundin, Nicholas Wolterstorff, Michael Straight, Chris Eberle, Terence Cuneo, David Sikkink, Sally Gallagher, Robert Woodberry, George Thomas, Alden Sunnaborg, Melinda Lundquist Denton, Kraig Beyerlein, Mike Welch, David Yamane, Mike Jindra, John Roth, Mark Regnerus, George Van Campbell, Marji Gunnoe, Michael Emerson, Kathy Miller, Keith Meador, Ben Zeller, Richard Wood, Michael Young, Penny Edgell, Lisa Pearce, Rhys Williams, two anonymous reviewers for Oxford University Press, and students in my fall 2002 "Religion and Society" class. I am very grateful to the University of Notre Dame for organizing a funded collaborative team sociology program, and to Calvin College for inviting me to lead a summer faculty seminar, both on the theme of "Morality, Culture, and the Power of Religion in Social Life," which provided extremely helpful contexts facilitating my thinking about and work on the arguments in this book. Thanks specifically to Nathan Hatch, Michael Hamilton, Kurt Berends, Susan Felch, and Joel Carpenter for their support in this regard. Both of the Notre Dame and Calvin College programs were funded by The Pew Charitable Trusts. Obviously, the positions argued in this book are my own and do not necessarily reflect those of The Pew Charitable Trusts. Closer to home, I am thankful to many people at the University of North Carolina's Howard W. Odum Institute for Research in Social Science for their very helpful assistance and support in administering the grant through the Notre Dame program: Ken Bollen, Charif Soubra, Beverly Wood, and Peter Leousis. Melinda Lundquist Denton has also been a superb graduate student assistant supporting my work. Thanks to all of you. Even closer to home, and most important, a million thanks to Emily, Zachary, Erin, and Caroline for your love and support.

CONTENTS

MORAL, BELIEVING ANIMALS

ONE

INTRODUCTION

What kind of animals are human beings? How can we describe their peculiar characteristics in a way that might improve, or at least enlarge, our understanding of human social action and institutions? This book explores one approach to answering these questions, developing a descriptive anthropology of human personhood from a particular sociological perspective.

My focus of inquiry here is age-old—what earlier writers might have called the question of "human nature" or "the human condition." Use of such terms may present a stumbling block for some readers I wish to engage, particularly those wary of essentialistic claims about human beings. So I generally avoid them. But there is no getting around the fact that this essay ultimately presumes that the animals we call human beings share an identifiable and peculiar set of capacities and proclivities that distinguishes them significantly from other animals on this planet.[1] Despite the vast differences in humanity between cultures and across history, no matter how differently people narrate their lives and histories, there remains an underlying structure of human personhood that helps

1. For an interesting anthropological counter to antiessentialism regarding human beings, see Donald Brown, *Human Universals* (New York: McGraw-Hill, 1991).

to order human culture, history, and narration. Or so I believe and will argue, despite how unfashionable such ideas may be in certain circles these days.

Nothing developed in this book is new or original. It has all been said before by other diverse thinkers in various ways. But in the course of carrying on collective discussions over time about interesting and important matters, it is sometimes helpful to have distinct positions restated anew. Even if we never finally resolve the differences or solve the problems, we may at least be able to move together to what an old friend of mine used to call "deeper levels of confusion." In that spirit, I argue in what follows that we have not really come to terms with human beings— ourselves—until we come to understand human persons as fundamentally moral, believing animals.

All of this, I will argue, has important implications for our theorizing of culture and social action. One of the main themes developed in the following pages is the need for any adequate theory of culture and action to provide a clear account of human motivations for social action. Although human motivations need not be the explicit focus of any particular theory or analysis, I will suggest that every theory and analysis inevitably does in fact assume some account of human motivations, and that we will do well to acknowledge and evaluate these assumptions. Analytical stories that attempt to ignore or deny the question of human motivations for action simply will not work—they end up incomplete at best and completely implausible at worst.

A second theme that will emerge in this work is that too much recent theorizing about culture and action in sociology has been very unhelpfully beset by overreactions against real but correctable flaws and oversimplifications in previous theories. This has resulted in unnecessary intellectual pendulum swings and bandwagon-like theoretical trends that have merely generated new flaws and oversimplifications themselves needing correction. In an effort, for example, both to dispose of the corpse and to banish the ghost of Talcott Parsons, we have to our disadvantage needlessly deprived ourselves of a number of insights that Parsons provided—however deficiently and cryptically he provided them. Better thus to reclaim and renovate the partial good in Parsons in light of what we have since learned than to handicap ourselves theoretically in our collective academic purity rituals of resisting contamination by the Parsonian legacy.

Along the way in this book, I will attempt to engage critically alternative theories of culture and human action, in order to try to clarify and develop the approach advanced here. This work is motivated in part by a dissatisfaction with a number of accounts of human culture and action that are current and influential in sociology. This work will succeed if it manages to make clear some of the fundamental problems that may be built into these accounts and to begin to explain an alternative approach that helps to solve those problems within the parameters of its own account.

In all of this, I am heavily indebted to some very interesting and important work in recent philosophy. One way to read this book is as an attempt to bring what I consider to be important insights in recent moral philosophy and epistemology to bear on versions of sociological thinking that strike me as badly in need of them. If this book succeeds, I expect that it will prompt us to take ourselves both less seriously in certain ways and much more seriously in others, for it suggests, I hope the reader sees, that there is both much less and much more at stake in the living of our lives than we perhaps normally think.

This book elaborates a descriptive anthropology of human personhood in the hope of enhancing our understanding of human social action and institutions. Some of the claims in this essay will strike some readers as reminiscent of antique notions of "human nature." So be it. All plausible theories of human action make controlling assumptions, whether implicit or explicit, about human personhood. Better to surface these assumptions so that they may be owned and debated rather than simply to deny their existence and operation. In any case, I intend this essay to contribute specifically to theoretical discussions in the sociology of culture, about what it means that humans are cultural beings and why that matters sociologically. I also attempt to offer what I hope will be some helpful ideas for thinking sociologically about religion. More generally, I hope to advance, despite this book's many loose ends, unresolved debates, and unexplored implications, a plausible argument about human persons—about ourselves—toward the immodest end of clearer, more realistic self-understanding.

TWO

HUMAN CULTURE(S) AS MORAL ORDER(S)

The ideas of culture and action are central in sociology and social theory. But what do we need from a theory of culture that will adequately explain human action and account for the complexities of the human experience? We need a theory of culture specifying the means by which people construct strategies of action, but also culture as providing the normative ends toward which people act. We need a theory of culture that recognizes the powerful influences on human action of forces that do not operate directly through human consciousness and intention, but also of forces that importantly motivate human action through consciously held ideas, beliefs, and commitments. And we need a theory of culture that accounts for the very real operation of rationally self-interested choice in human life, but also the pervasive and powerful human enacted affirmations of moral commitments that are not reducible to self-interest.

In what follows I argue that the most adequate approach to theorizing human culture must be a normative one that conceives of humans as moral, believing animals and human social life as consisting of moral orders that constitute and direct social action. Human culture is always moral order. Human cultures are everywhere moral orders. Human persons are nearly inescapably moral agents. Human actions are necessarily morally constituted and propelled practices. And human institutions are inevitably morally infused configurations of rules and resources.

Moral Animals

One of the central and fundamental motivations for human action is to act out and sustain moral order, which helps constitute, directs, and makes significant human life itself. Human persons nearly universally live in social worlds that are thickly webbed with moral assumptions, beliefs, commitments, and obligations. The relational ties that hold human lives together, the conversations that occupy people's mental lives, the routines and intentions that shape their actions, the institutions within which they live and work, the emotions they feel every day—all of these and more are drenched in, patterned by, glued together with moral premises, convictions, and obligations. These morally constituted and permeated worlds exist outside of people, in structured social practices and relationships within which people's lives are embedded. They also exist "inside" of people, in their assumptions, expectations, beliefs, aspirations, thoughts, judgments, and feelings. There is nowhere a human can go to escape moral order. There is no way to be human except through moral order.

What I mean by "moral," to be clear, is an orientation toward understandings about what is right and wrong, good and bad, worthy and unworthy, just and unjust, that are not established by our own actual desires, decisions, or preferences but instead believed to exist apart from them, providing standards by which our desires, decisions, and preferences can themselves be judged.[1] Human animals are moral animals in that we possess a capacity and propensity unique among all animals: we not only have desires, beliefs, and feelings (which often have strong moral qualities) but also the ability and disposition to form strong evaluations about our

---

1. Here I very closely follow Charles Taylor, who describes morality as involving "discriminations of right and wrong, better or worse, higher or lower, which are not rendered valid by our own desires, inclinations, or choices, but rather stand independently of these and offer standards by which they can be judged." Taylor, *Sources of the Self* (Cambridge: Harvard University Press, 1989), 4. In these pages, I use the term "normative" somewhat more broadly than the term "moral," insofar as the normative includes systems directing behavior—such as customs, mores, protocols, etiquettes, and so on—that do not always convey the stronger sense of the moral as defined here. The culturally moral is thus a conceptual subset of the culturally normative.

desires, beliefs, and feelings that hold the potential to transform them. The Canadian philosopher Charles Taylor refers to this as having "second order desires"—desires *about* our desires.[2] Humans not only have the ability to hate, for instance, but also the ability to judge that our hatreds are wrong and to come to the place where we do not *want* any more to be hateful. It is not simply that we first hate and then our hatred fades. It is that even while we are still hating we can form the desire not to hate, because of evaluative judgments we make about our hate. Hatred is the first order desire, the wish not to hate is the second order desire—a desire about another desire.

Note that people do not always form second order desires, nor do they always succeed in achieving them when they do. Some people sometimes hate without compunction. Others who wish not to be hateful cannot move beyond their hatred. Still, people normally do incessantly make strong evaluations about their thoughts, emotions, and wants that have the potential to revise them on moral grounds. A man may have an uncontrollably gluttonous desire to eat but may also feel profound shame for his complete lack of ingestive self-control (and not only his obesity), and so very strongly desires to become a person who is temperate and self-controlled in his eating. Likewise, a wife may no longer feel much love for her husband but believes for a variety of reasons that it is right to love him anyway (besides her not wishing to suffer the adverse consequences, such as divorce, of continuing not to love him) and so comes actually to desire to love her husband (even though she now does not) and then takes steps to try to rekindle her love for him. This process can engage beliefs as well as desires. For example, a white person who may have since childhood held deep down in his heart the racist belief that blacks and Hispanics are inferior to whites may have recently come to the conviction that racism is just plain wrong; in which case, he may then form the strong desire to get rid of the deep-seated racist beliefs that he

---

2. Charles Taylor, *Human Agency and Language* (Cambridge: Cambridge University Press, 1985). Taylor here is following H. Frankfurt, "Freedom of the Will and the Concept of the Person," *Journal of Philosophy* 67, no. 1 (January 1971): 5–20. One might question whether what Taylor calls second order desires are actually *desires*, or whether they might more accurately be called judgments or evaluations.

knows he still in fact holds. All of these cases involve moral judgments of self—strong evaluations based on external standards of good and bad, right and wrong, virtue and vice, and so on, that transform the fundamental question from "What do I want?" and "How do I feel?" and "What do I believe?" into "What should I want?" and "How ought I to feel?" and "What is the right thing to believe?" Human collective moral order and action are founded on and sustain this distinctive human proclivity toward forming second order desires based on strong evaluations of first order desires, beliefs, and feelings. What I mean by "moral order," to be explicit, is intersubjectively and institutionally shared social structurings of moral systems that are derived from the larger narratives and belief systems described in the following two chapters.

Thus when an action or order is moral, in this sense, it entails an imperative to affirm a commitment to shared rules or obligations that apply to people in certain defined situations and statuses. The moral also involves a sense of normative duty to express or perform obligations that are intrinsically motivated—because they are right, good, worthy, just, and so on—rather than motivated by the means/ends-oriented desire to obtain the benefit of consuming a good or service.[3]

The stranger thus acts morally when she finds on a deserted sidewalk a wallet full of lots of money, goes home, calls its owner, and returns the wallet with all of its contents. To do otherwise would itself be dishonest and uncaring—even if it would make her richer without anyone else knowing. The citizen acts morally when he gets up after dinner and goes out in the pouring rain to cast his vote as one among tens of millions of votes in an election. To do otherwise would be bad citizenship—even if in most cases his one vote could make no difference in any electoral outcome. In these and all like cases, actions are performed at least in part because they affirm and express commitments to what are understood to be right, good, worthy, just, and so on. And these are understood to entail imperatives independent of the actor's own personal wishes and inclinations, and not because they might achieve some other valued outcome or benefit. The basic difference here in terms of philosophical ethics is be-

3. In this I am following Amitai Etzioni, *The Moral Dimension* (New York: Free Press, 1988), 41–45.

tween deontological and teleological ethical systems; virtue ethics also comports with the sense of morality I develop here, and so do, arguably, certain versions of nonutilitarian consequentialist ethics.

But actions and practices are not all that are moral in human social life. Social institutions and cultural systems, the next section suggests, are also always moral in this sense. For the stranger returning a wallet full of money as an individual act is itself necessarily embedded within a larger shared cultural system specifying particular norms, values, virtues, ethics, and notions of the human good toward which any good person ought to aspire. The action of the good citizen who votes in every election no matter what the weather only makes sense within a larger institutional framework of political democracy that itself is constituted by normative definitions and beliefs about freedom, participation, self-governance, public virtue, political legitimacy, procedural fairness, and so on.

What I am claiming here is that to enact and sustain moral order is one of the central, fundamental motivations for human action;[4] and that until this is recognized and built into our theories and analyses, our understanding of human action and culture will be impoverished.[5]

---

4. Motivation is often defined as the process of activating, directing, and maintaining behavior or action, which psychologists typically differentiate into internal and external motivations, both aspects of which the following argument incorporates.

5. Here I pick up on that aspect of Robert Wuthnow's cultural sociology that highlights the centrality of moral order in human social life. Thus, in *Meaning and Moral Order* (Cambridge: Harvard University Press, 1987), 346, Wuthnow observed, "Social relations require some degree of organization and . . . this organization is not supplied in all cases either by totally coercive power structures or by totally self-interested exchanges of goods and services. Even in coercive and self-interested exchanges of goods and services, signals need to be sent about actors' positions and the course of action they are likely to take. The signals constitute, on the one hand, the moral order and are, on the other hand, supplied by the cultural forms such as ideology and rituals." At this point, Durkheimians may suggest that humans are moral simply because they are social, and the social is the essential source of the moral. This book's argument is friendly to an intimate connection between the social and the moral—see, for example, the discussion below under "Some Implications"—but seeks to ground the moral more specifi-

What I do *not* mean in saying that humans are motivated to enact and sustain moral order is that people always act morally, that they consistently live up to their own and others' moral standards. People clearly do not. In fact people can, for a variety of reasons, routinely violate all sorts of moral convictions and normative codes. To say that human persons are moral beings is a statement about an externally and subjectively patterned human situation, not a statement about consistent individual behavior within that situation.

Many cases of moral dereliction themselves typically reflect the functioning of a larger, intact, powerful moral order at work. For one thing, people often feel guilty about their wrongdoings, recognizing some moral culpability for failing to live up to moral standards. In so doing, they continue to live within, to reference, and to affirm backhandedly the validity of the larger moral order. Furthermore, certain moral compromises and failures are the outcomes of tensions between what are experienced as conflicting moral demands. A student lies to a teacher about her boyfriend painting graffiti on the wall because she thinks it is (morally) wrong for girlfriends to betray boyfriends' trust in that way. A father repeatedly breaks his promises to come see his daughter's soccer games because he feels compelled to fulfill his obligations as a good employee at work to ensure that he will always be the good provider for his family that he believes he should be.

This is not to say that rationalizations and self-deceptions are not also often at work in these cases; simply that violations of morals, rather than negating the reality of moral order, often transpire with reference to the constraints and contradictions of complex moral systems. Otherwise, we would have no concept or practice of rationalization itself. For people only ever need to rationalize behaviors when they and their audiences share understandings of moral orders within which their behaviors are questionable. A CEO may choose to lay off four hundred employees one week before Christmas because it will play very well for his career at the all-important February board of trustees meeting; yet he tells himself and his tennis partner that this is really, if unfortunately, the right thing to do

---

cally in something closer to the operation of "human nature," and not simply as a product of collective social relations, than may be comfortable for some Durkheimian theorists.

since it will consolidate company strength and create more jobs over the long run. Why? Only because this CEO lives within and to some extent must live up to a normative order that says that a good person does not put others out of jobs just before Christmas. If many people did not significantly truly believe in such moral orders, they would never feel the need to rationalize.

Moreover, some actions that violate shared standards of morality result partly from the disjunct between the external and subjective aspects of moral order. An eighteen-year-old boy has sex with his drunk and reluctant fifteen-year-old date (violating statutory rape laws and norms against date rape) not simply because of raw, hormonal sex drive but also because he actually believes, in a complex adolescent moral order of romance and sex, that she had provocatively "led him on" in a way that gave him the (moral) right to have her. Internalized moral orders do not perfectly mirror external moral orders, so actions based on normative assumptions operating at one level can work to violate norms at another level. In some cases, gross moral violations may actually reflect the faithful upholding of alternative moral orders. For example, a brutal revenge murder by mob hit men set in motion by a Mafia family is not likely to be a random act of irrationality or a mere instrumental move to secure material advantage. Rather, it is the discharging of solemn duties to uphold a certain moral order involving honor, self-respect, and vindication. The majority of us may abhor the Mafia's particular moral order (as we do the date rape)— because we live within other moral orders—but that does not alter the morally charged character of the revenge murder or the normatively informed motivations of those who ordered it.

There may be very rare exceptions to the morally constituted and infused character of human persons: the relatively few people we call sociopaths, or psychopaths—those who have the clinical diagnosis "antisocial personality disorder." These people lack consciences, routinely disregard social norms, feel no empathy for others, and are treacherously manipulative, destructive, and remorseless for the damage they inflict on others. Sociopaths are people who seem to live amoral lives, who cannot or will not recognize that they inhabit a shared moral order that makes binding claims on them (although they do often closely follow their own rules, their own moral orders). Notorious among these are Ted Bundy and Charles Manson. For my purposes, however, it is important to see that sociopaths are exceptions that prove the rule about human moral order. We label them as sick, as abnormal, as repulsive deviants. When their remorselessly destructive ways become publicly known, we feel deep revulsion for them and lock them behind bars. We know that something has gone very deeply wrong with their humanity, that even though they are genetically human, they have become in a sense somehow something *less than human.* Thus while individual persons without any shared moral compass or conscience occasionally can and do surface in society, we experience them as somehow inhuman, as outside the bounds of humanity. And the complex machinery of the larger human moral order within which the sociopath lives then moves to capture, judge, and cage or kill them. And what remains intact as normal and controlling is the thickly webbed moral world of human society.

It is useful in this discussion not to confuse morality with "altruism." In the course of background research for writing this essay, I studied a number of social psychology textbooks, where I was surprised to discover little if any attention paid to morality or moral order. Social psychology, it appears, has no clue about humans as moral animals but appears to prefer to think of humans as mere cognitive information processors. Close scrutiny of their tables of contents and indexes yields few if any references to morality. Most texts, however, did devote—in what seemed to be a spirit of obligatory coverage—one page or two to the subject of altruism. Do people ever sacrifice their own interests for the welfare of others? If so, what kind of people, and under what conditions do they do so? The typical textbook example focused on those who risked their own safety to rescue Jews from the Nazis. However interesting studies of altruism are, and however important it is to establish that humans can and do act altruistically, morality in the ways I am discussing it here cannot be reduced to altruism. Altruism, among humans at least, is a particular attitudinal and behavioral expression of a certain kind of moral commitment that becomes relevant in specific situations within systems of moral order. But morality, as described here, is much bigger, thicker, and more complex than mere altruism. Most versions of human altruism could not exist without morality.[6] But there are all kinds of moral beliefs,

---

6. Some animals that do not appear to possess the moral faculties discussed in this chapter seem to display behaviors that we think of as altruistic, and this

judgments, and actions that are not particularly altruistic. One's actions can be normatively directed in many ways without the action being self-sacrificial. One can live in relation to what one understands to be the good, the right, the true, the just without that always involving the self-less concern for others' welfare. To suppose then that taking morality seriously essentially means paying closer attention to altruism both unrealistically raises the bar on and drastically narrows the range of what might count as moral.

Human emotions provide excellent telltale indicators of the moral assumptions, convictions, and expectations that pervade and order our personal and collective lives. A son feels guilt for not taking care of his ailing, aged mother in a way he knows a good son should. A wife feels annoyed that her husband spends the weekend watching sports on television when he could be painting the house or talking with her about her week. A grandfather feels deeply thankful at his youngest granddaughter's baptism, knowing that his family is turning out just right. An employee feels angry for not getting the raise she thought her boss had promised and that she clearly deserves. The party host feels embarrassed in front of their guests by the rude misbehavior shown by their teenage kids. A clique of university students is elated to hear that the professor they had for a class who was a terrible lecturer and an unfair grader was denied tenure. A parent is outraged on learning that her school district hired a felon for a janitor without first checking on his record and references. A father feels profound contentment when his daughter eagerly takes over the family business that he started and built up over the last thirty-five years. A girl feels betrayed when she learns that the boy she was dating "exclusively" has also been seeing another girl. Passersby feel indifferent to a homeless beggar they suspect is a self-destructive drug addict. A religious group is offended when leaders of another religion organize to proselytize its members. A nation's people is shocked by the unprovoked attack of a neighboring country and rallies to prepare for war. These emotions and most others are signs of moral orders fulfilled and moral orders violated. They serve as clues of often unarticulated, assumed beliefs about and commit-

---

altruism appears to have a genetic basis. See below, however, the discussion on sociobiology as an inadequate explanation of human moral commitments and actions.

ments to normative expectations embedded in larger moral systems within which people make sense of and live out their lives.

Human social life is well understood as the "liturgy" of moral order. Religious liturgies—as with, for instance, the liturgical worship styles of the Catholic, Orthodox, and Anglican churches—are the collective enactments, the dramatic ritualizations of the theological stories of faith traditions. Liturgy is the work of a congregation that expresses, performs, and represents a sacred narrative through song, prayer, reading, confession, consecration, proclamation, procession, silence, kneeling, standing, candle lighting, incense burning, bread breaking, and more. Liturgy ritually reenacts a tradition, an experience, a history, a worldview. It expresses in dramatic and corporeal form a sacred belief system in words, music, imagery, aromas, tastes, and bodily movement. In liturgy, worshipers both perform and observe, act out truth and have the truth act on them, remember the past and carry it into the future. Liturgy expresses, professes, performs, and informs. This is what religious liturgies do. It is also exactly what human social life more generally does with cultural moral order. All of the social practices, relations, and institutions that comprise human social life generally themselves together dramatize, ritualize, proclaim, and reaffirm the moral order that constitutes social life. Moral order embodies the sacred story of the society, however profane it appears, and the social actors are believers in social congregation. Together they remember, recite, represent, and reaffirm the normative structure of their moral order. All of the routines, habits, and conventions of micro interaction ritualize what they know about the good, the right, the true, the just. All of the systems and structures of macro institutional life do likewise. This is simply the way of moral, believing animals.

The ethnomethodological experiments of the sociologist Harold Garfinkel and his followers in the 1960s and 1970s are just one example that makes this clear. Garfinkel was interested in the delicate order of human micro interactions, particularly the precarious yet resilient interactional structures that regulate interpersonal conversations. Garfinkel and his students uncovered the standards and boundaries of these orders through the use of "breaching experiments" that intentionally violated the norms and conventions of conversation in order to observe people's responses. On the phone, for example, when people said, "Hello, how are you?" the ethnomethodologists replied, "What do you mean, 'How am I'?" At first, people quickly worked to repair the breakdown, but the ethnomethodologists continued to refuse to cooperate. What they discovered in the process was not only how easily simple conversations can be disrupted but how vehemently people reacted to these disruptions. At first, their interaction partners were simply completely confused. Rather quickly, however, they became hostile, indignant, angry. "What do you mean, 'What do you mean, "How am I"?'! What is your problem!?" People, Garfinkel reports, were not simply frustrated, they were outraged.[7] For, we can observe, their elementary rules facilitating the enactment of moral order were being violated. Garfinkel was not only being difficult; he was interrupting and desecrating the liturgy of social life. What he did was sociologically parallel to standing up in the middle of Catholic mass to burp loudly and shout obscenities. It was simply something nobody does, and when Garfinkel did, it incurred people's wrath.

One of the well-known moves that neoclassical economics and social exchange and rational choice theories make is to shift analytical attention away from variability in people's "preferences and values" and to focus instead on the rationally calculated choices of self-interested actors. Either people's preferences are assumed to be stable and common (i.e., to maximize material gain) or they are readily bracketed off from investigation with the simple phrase "given people's values and preferences . . ." A standard critique of these approaches that I reiterate here is that social science simply cannot neglect preferences and values. For one thing, they clearly are not stable and common. For another, they simply cannot be bracketed as an analytical "given." If anything, it is the rationality, calculation, and choice that might be bracketed from analysis, since the real variance and interesting explanatory punch is so often not found there but in the variance in preferences, values, and commitments of the actors. And this is why finally any good sociological analysis is and needs self-consciously to

7. See Harold Garfinkel, *Studies in Ethnomethodology* (Englewood Cliffs, N.J.: Prentice Hall, 1967), 42–44; also see Harvey Sacks, Emanuel Schegloff, and Gail Jefferson, "A Simplest Systematics for the Organization of Turn-taking for Conversation," *Language* 50 (1974): 696–735. Thanks to George Thomas for pointing out this connection to my argument.

be a cultural sociology.[8] Even purely quantitative sociology using advanced statistical techniques must finally engage in cultural sociology, insofar as for quantitative sociology to make any sense, the meaning and effects of its variables must in the end be explained and interpreted in terms of their cultural significance and influence in social life—"findings" and tables are always followed by "discussion," which nearly always relies, at least implicitly, on cultural interpretation. Sex, education, income, race, region, marital status, religion, neighborhood composition, and nearly every other variable in bivariate tables and multivariate models are usually social facts that significantly associate with social effects because of the cultural meanings they have in people's lives and the social influences they therefore exert. Indeed, it is precisely the job of cultural analysis in these cases, whether done persuasively or badly, and consciously so or not, to turn observed significant associations into plausible causal influences in the minds of journal article readers.

For my purposes, however, the key point is more specific than this broad claim. It is that preferences and valuings are typically and perhaps nearly always powerfully shaped by, if not derived from, larger systems of moral order. Preferences are not primarily self-referential inclinations. And values are not abstract, free-floating personal appraisals. Both preferences and values involve reference to discriminations between worthy and unworthy, good and bad, right and wrong, truth and falsehood, and so on. They are socially normative and evaluative dispositions. Few people value individual freedom, for example, simply because they personally and idiosyncratically so happen to value it. People value freedom because they are embedded in a larger moral order that specifies what is good, right, true, just, and worthy in the context of which freedom is prized. Note that not all people in history or across cultures have valued or do value individual freedom as many Americans, for example, do. That is because they inhabit other, different moral orders within which freedom is less highly regarded. Likewise, some people's preference for lethargic beach vacations spent basking in the sun and sipping margaritas—as opposed to, say, vacations spent scaling mountain peaks or gambling at Vegas or in social service projects in poor communities—are not random, con-

8. See Margaret Archer and Jonathan Tritter, *Rational Choice Theory: Resisting Colonization* (New York: Routledge, 2000).

textless fancies. Rather, the lazy beach vacation preference is generated by and draws meaning from a larger moral order specifying a particular account of "the good life" involving particular normative notions of self, health, work, leisure, pleasure, and reward. In sum, explaining differences in preferences and values is a crucial element of sociological analysis, and preferences and values can only be explained in terms of the moral orders from which they arise, in which they are embedded, and that suffuse them with meaning.

Here is precisely the point where we can observe the trouble that some social scientists have run into in the use of the idea of social norms. In some cases, scholars have employed the idea of norms as if they were free-floating bits of behavioral expectations governing self and others. Jon Elster, for instance, writes persuasively on social norms in *The Cement of Society* that certain human actions simply cannot be explained as intending to minimize costs and maximize benefits to self. Rather, he argues, some types of action are clearly norm following.[9] That is an important observation. Yet Elster leaves the reader with the impression that norms are essentially autonomous packets of action-directives, rather arbitrary and specific instructions that specify very particular lines of action. One simply does not ask one's adult neighbor whether they would be willing to mow one's lawn for pay. One does not flagrantly pick one's nose in public, even in front of complete strangers who cannot sanction you and whom you will never see again. One does not walk up to someone waiting in line to purchase theater tickets and offer to buy their place in line. "It simply isn't done," Elster observes. But what Elster appears to be missing in this otherwise persuasive exposition is the degree to which social norms

---

9. Jon Elster, *The Cement of Society: A Study of Social Order* (Cambridge: Cambridge University Press, 1989), quotes from pp. 111, 125. Of course, acting to minimize costs and maximize benefits is typically itself the following of norms. Also see Michael Hechter, "Values Research in the Social and Behavioral Sciences," in Michael Hechter, Lynn Nadel, and Richard Michod (eds.), *The Origin of Values* (New York: Aldine de Gruyter, 1993); Antony S. R. Manstead, "The Role of Moral Norm in the Attitude-Behavior Relation," in Deborah Ferry and Michael Hogg (eds.), *Attitude, Behavior, and Social Context* (Mahwah, N.J.: Lawrence Erlbaum Associates, 2000); and James Spates, "The Sociology of Values," *Annual Review of Sociology* 9 (1983): 27–49.

are tied to larger moral orders in relation to which they make sense and carry influence. He quite frankly confesses, "I cannot offer a positive explanation of norms. I do not know why human beings have a propensity to construct and follow norms, nor how specific norms come into being." Although it might not be obvious on the surface, I suggest that discrete social norms are usually linked to larger, complicated normative systems that carry some weight of history and tradition, that are meaningful in terms of some believed narrative. Most people avoid indiscreetly picking their noses on the subway, for instance, not because some arbitrary and free-floating bit of behavioral directive for whatever reason says not to. Rather, they do not pick their noses because their lives are embedded in and carried along by what Norbert Elias has shown is a much larger civilizing process that has developed culturally over many centuries in the West that elaborates a complex normative order of dignity, privacy, propriety, and shame that profoundly governs the comportment of our public lives.[10] If so, one of the jobs of sociologists must be not simply to demonstrate the continued influence of social norms in human action but to explicate the cultural history, substance, texture, and significance of the larger, more complex moral orders within which specific social norms are generated and operate.

Morally Animated Institutions

One of the long-standing false dichotomies in sociological theory has been "culture" versus "society"—the intangible ideas, values, and beliefs of a people (culture) counterposed against supposedly more real or hard social institutions (society). This ultimately unhelpful distinction has closely paralleled other false dichotomies in social theory: agency versus structure, freedom versus constraint, ideal versus material. These mistaken distinctions have generated endless arguments between idealists and materialists, culturalists and structuralists, humanists and determinists, and more.

Fortunately, social theory in recent years has seen a tremendously helpful rethinking of these issues. This reconsideration has invalidated many

10. Norbert Elias, *The History of Manners* (New York: Pantheon, 1982) and *The Civilizing Process* (Cambridge: Blackwell, 1994).

of the old, misleading dichotomies by showing how thoroughly cultural social structures and institutions are and how entirely dependent on material resources culture is. Particularly helpful in this matter have been the separate works of Anthony Giddens and William H. Sewell Jr.[11] They conceive of social structures as complex systems of rules and resources (Giddens) or schema and resources (Sewell). This means that society and all of its institutions and structures are always constituted in part by mental categories and maps that serve as cultural classifications that order the distribution and deployment of resources. Of course, the rules or schema are also themselves significantly shaped by the distribution of resources, since ideas are not free-floating entities but require institutions to sustain and promote them. But what is clearly not the case is the old idea that society and institutions are somehow real, hard, substantial, determinative while ideas, beliefs, and consciousness are somehow more ephemeral, superficial, and derivative. Every version of the classical infrastructure-superstructure distinction is a false dichotomy. Instead, every social system, structure, and institution is always and necessarily constituted and defined by cultural rules or schemas that make it more or less meaningful and legitimate; and every cultural rule or schema depends on systems of material and nonmaterial resources to be sustained. Thus society apart from culture, if that is even possible to imagine, is like the body without a living spirit (for those still able to think in those terms)—it is dead, an empty array of objects without any purpose, orienting motivation, or legitimacy.

What these theoretical insights help us to see, for the purposes of this essay, is the intimate connection between moral order and social institu-

---

11. William H. Sewell Jr., "A Theory of Structure: Duality, Agency, and Transformation," *American Journal of Sociology* 98 (1992): 1–29; also see William H. Sewell Jr., "The Concept(s) of Culture," in Victoria Bonnell and Lynn Hunt (eds.), *Beyond the Cultural Turn: New Directions in the Study of Society and Culture*, 35–61 (Berkeley: University of California Press, 1999); Anthony Giddens, *Central Problems in Social Theory* (Berkeley: University of California Press, 1979); Giddens, *The Constitution of Society* (Berkeley: University of California Press, 1984); also see Sharon Hays, "Structure and Agency and the Sticky Problem of Culture," *Sociological Theory* 12, no. 1 (1994): 57–72. For an alternative approach, see Margaret Archer, *Realist Social Theory* (New York: Cambridge University Press, 1995).

tions. The moral is not simply a subjective concern limited to religion, ethical rules, or personal values. Nor are institutions merely practical arrangements for the accomplishing of functional tasks, like delivering health care and making political decisions. Rather, social institutions are always morally animated enterprises. All social institutions are embedded within and give expression to moral orders that generate, define, and govern them. Whether it is obvious on surface appearances or not, social institutions are inevitably rooted in and expressions of the narratives, traditions, and worldviews of moral orders.[12]

Universities, for example, are not simply practical systems for producing research findings and increasing human capital in students in order functionally to strengthen a state's economy. Universities are more fundamentally stable configurations of resources (buildings, personnel, budgets, reputations, and so on) grounded in and reproducing moral order. American universities, for instance, are expressive incarnations of certain moral narratives, traditions, and commitments concerning the good, the right, and the true regarding human development, student character, the nature of knowledge, the purposes of education, equality and merit, academic freedom, liberal arts and technical training, racial justice, gender relations, socioeconomic background, collegial decision-making, the place of the arts, the limits of religion, the informed consent of human subjects, the value of sports, and so on. And these, of course, are themselves rooted in even deeper moral traditions and worldviews about the nature of human personhood, epistemologies, historical progress, liberty and equality, legitimate authority, and more. It does not matter that some students, faculty, administrators, or trustees may not understand their universities as grounded in and expressive of particular moral order. It does not normally even matter that some or many of them may actually disagree with the moral traditions, narratives, or worldviews animating their university. For these individuals are embedded in the larger institution whose purpose it is to express and reproduce the moral order that animates it, which is older and bigger than any individual or group of individuals. The institution lives on, more thoroughly shaping people in its image than being reshaped by movements of people's alternative moral imaginations.

---

12. See Robert Bellah, Richard Madsen, William Sullivan, Ann Swidler, and Steven Tipton, *The Good Society* (New York: Alfred A. Knopf, 1991), 287–93.

The same case could be made of all other social institutions, including those involving politics, courtship, marriage, family, law, science, health care, the media, education, recreation, the military, social services, business and industry, or any other socially structured human activity. Behind, beneath, in, and through all of the institutions involved in these human practices are moral orders rooted in historical narratives, traditions, and worldviews that orient human actors to the good, the right, the true. For human persons are fundamentally and inescapably moral and believing animals who cannot grow, live, or act apart from moral bearings. Sometimes the moral order animating institutions becomes too big, too dominant, too obvious to recognize—even, or perhaps especially, for educated, modern people. But this does not mean moral order is not operative, rather that it is all the more powerfully operative.

But surely, some may protest, the capitalist marketplace at least is a sphere of human activity devoid of moral consideration and governance. In it individuals calculate, bargain, buy, and sell only to maximize their material self-interest. The market is all and only about free exchange and economic profit. And the laws of supply and demand are so bloodless that the "creative destruction" of market capitalism is often cruel and ruthless. Where is there any moral order in that? In fact, numerous observers have shown definitively that market capitalism too is thoroughly engendered by and expressive of moral order.[13] The capitalist market is no neutral space or amoral institution. It presumes a particular, normative notion of human persons as basically rational, materially acquisitive, and

13. See, for example, Wuthnow, *Meaning and Moral Order*, 79–95; Paul DiMaggio, "Cultural Aspects of Economic Action and Organization," in Roger Friedland and A. F. Robertson (eds.), *Beyond the Marketplace*, 113–36 (New York: Aldine de Gruyter, 1990); George Thomas, *Revivalism and Cultural Change* (Chicago: University of Chicago Press, 1989); Jane Mansbridge (ed.), *Beyond Self-Interest* (Chicago: University of Chicago Press, 1990); Viviana Zelizer, "The Social Meaning of Money," *American Journal of Sociology* 95, no. 2 (1989): 342–77; Viviana Zelizer, *The Social Meaning of Money* (New York: Basic Books, 1994); Karl Polanyi, *The Great Transformation* (Boston: Beacon Press, 1957). Also see Julie Brines, "Economic Dependency, Gender, and the Division of Labor at Home," *American Journal of Sociology* 100, no. 3 (1994): 652–88, for an example of how cultural logics of gender override economic logics of exchange.

self-interested. It stakes out a particular moral position on matters of human need, responsibility, equality, freedom, welfare, and merit. It is linked to specific normative commitments about property ownership, entrepreneurial initiative, the deferred gratification of consumption, and often liberal democracy. Furthermore, the market is no self-generating, autonomous entity but only exists because (morally animated) political, legal, and regulatory structures and interventions sustain it—just as these were also required to sustain other kinds of economic systems throughout history. So a landlord may feel that morality has nothing to do with his renting a house in the mountains to a wealthy couple to use it occasionally as a summer cottage rather than to a struggling, poor, local family who desperately needs shelter. But in fact a particular moral order most definitely animates the market institution within which his seemingly amoral action makes sense. And it is a moral order tied to specific, historical, normative traditions, narratives, and worldviews—especially Anglo, liberal individualism. All this becomes more obvious when one considers the particular alternative moral orders that have historically animated quite different economic institutions—for instance, lord-and-serf feudalism, colonial imperialism, communism, mercantilism, and slave-based economies—that are based on and express quite different moral notions of the state, human freedom, individual rights and responsibilities, the moral purposes of wealth, and so on.

But surely science at least is different from these other institutions? Science cannot be an incarnation of moral order, for morality is historical, particularistic, partial, and committed, whereas science is objective, universal, and based on fact, not faith. Is not science the one method that transcends human beliefs and biases and provides rational and impartial truth about reality? A seventeenth-century Hopi Native American might not think so. Neither might a Hindu monk living in Calcutta. Neither, for that matter, might have Albert Einstein. Without belaboring the point, suffice it to say that—for all the knowledge about the material and human world that science has generated, which has enhanced our technological ability to manipulate the living and inorganic world and alter our material standard of living—modern, Western science, like all institutions, is a set of practices that developed out of and express a distinct moral order comprising particular, historical narratives, traditions, and worldviews.

It clearly is grounded on and perpetuates particular assumptions and com-mitments—about matter, causality, regularity, human sensory observa-tion, quantification, and much more—that science itself cannot possibly justify and that have not been self-evident to all rational people every-where at all times. Science is also driven by distinct moral notions about what a good human life looks like, the nature and value of progress, the ethics of alliances with government and industry, the limits of its own moral culpability (for example, in developing weapons of mass destruction or cloning human beings), and so on. Science as we know it can only ever proceed by first placing faith in a set of unprovable cosmological, metaphysical, and epistemological assumptions and commitments.[14] And science as we know it proceeds by hitching its wagon to a set of nine-teenth-century general assumptions about civilization, progress, knowl-edge, and morality. Science may have put a man on the moon (which was itself a morally, politically, and emotionally pregnant endeavor). But we cannot say that science is exempt from the moral and believing character of human persons and society. Nothing human, not even science, escapes moral order.

One of the best ways to reveal the moral character of social institutions, as noted earlier, is to violate moral norms and observe the reactions. One quickly learns that one is not simply proposing an alternative idea but has profaned a moral commitment of sacred character. Try, for example, proposing that all American state university course curricula include teachings from the Bible relevant to each course's subject. Or try arguing among social scientists that empirically observed socioeconomic disparities between racial and ethnic groups are actually the result of inherent group genetic differences that determine one group to be better and more suc-cessful than another. Or venture to advocate that, in the interest of long-term societal well-being and rational human evolution, the government should systematically employ material incentives and forced sterility and abortions to limit the fertility of couples who have low IQs or physical blemishes or who belong to a particular religion or ethnicity. Or suggest

14. Michael Polanyi, *Science, Faith, and Society* (Chicago: University of Chicago Press, 1946), and *Personal Knowledge: Toward a Post-Critical Philosophy* (Chicago: University of Chicago Press, 1958).

in the lab that the research team starts each day by praying to the Creator for supernaturally provided insight into the problem under investigation.[15] At first you may be amusingly dismissed as nuts, unworthy of a serious response. But if your suggestion happens to come to be perceived as serious and as garnering some legitimacy, then agents of the relevant moral order will come down on you with fierce emotion and retribution to eradicate the desecrating offense to the moral order. This is simply the nature of social institutions grounded in the moral and sustained by animals who are most fundamentally moral and believing.

Some Implications

What all of this means for a theory of culture is that the moral order that motivates and shapes human action is not merely something internalized through socialization. Human action is wrongly understood as simply the external behavioral product, operating in neutral social space, of individuals' internal programming, directives, or specified ends. Rather, the moral order that generates and guides human action permeates all aspects of the social order within which human lives are embedded and from which human animals draw their identities and capacities. Moral order permeates human existence. It suffuses the structured configurations of resources and practices that comprise our organizations and institutions. Moral order is thus woven into, indeed defines, the very woven patterns of the social fabric itself. All of this then positions moral order as external to and objectively existent for human actors. At the same time, however, precisely because human actors are constituted, developed, propelled, and guided by the social institutions in which their lives are embedded, the moral orders animating social institutions also find imperfectly corre-

15. Here is an indication of the power of moral order and moral commitment: one sympathetic colleague who reviewed this book's manuscript worried that even my use of these examples of morally deviant ideas—particularly the one about genetic differences—would invite personal attributions and criticisms from readers assuming that I am somehow sympathetic to these views, which I am not, and suggested that I simply drop some of them. Thus even hypothetical illustrations for theoretical arguments may become morally loaded and potentially dangerous.

sponding expression *within* human actors—in the assumptions, ideas, values, beliefs, volitions, emotions, and so on of human subjectivity, conscience, consciousness, and self-consciousness. The human actors who both produce and are produced by social institutions thus engage moral order both objectively and subjectively. And the moral orders both inside and outside of human persons reflect and reproduce each other. This duality is lived in practice through a unified process that is historical, dialectical, and reciprocally self-reinforcing.

I have just spoken of the *imperfect* character of the internally corresponding expression of institutional moral order in human subjectivity. By this I recognize the recurrent disjunct between the moral orders animating social institutions and those that individuals internalize through socialization. There is a definite and strong correspondence between the two, but a correspondence that is nevertheless imperfect and somewhat mismatched. This is so for three reasons. The first is that any single moral order never develops in complete and seamless unity. There are always, as Sewell has pointed out, intellectual and practical cracks, loose ends, unclear boundaries, implementation difficulties, tensions, incongruities, and contradictions that beset any discrete system of moral order.[16] Never do the pieces of humanly constructed systems—however rational, systematic, or elegant—all fit together neatly and completely. There is therefore always room for wiggling, maneuvering, doubts, challenges, misunderstandings, and the consideration of and, possibly, conversion to alternative moral orders. Thus even as intellectually tight a theological system as Calvinism, for example, has various weak spots, unanswered questions, problematic implications, and—we know—defectors to Arminianism, Unitarianism, Deism, and various forms of secular political activism.

Second, rarely does any human social order encompass only one system of moral order. More likely, any conglomeration of social institutions that comprise what we call "society" are animated by many competing and blended moral orders. American culture, for example, has been observed to be an odd mingling of the biblical tradition, a republican tradition, utilitarian individualism, and expressive individualism—which together clash and amalgamate to produce the interesting Christian-capitalist-democratic-romanticist-libertarian-secular thing that is the United

16. Sewell, "A Theory of Structure" and "The Concept(s) of Culture."

States.[17] Some moral orders tend to be restrictive and discriminating in relation to others, while yet others can be quite promiscuous. But no moral order is entirely impervious to the influence of other moral orders with which it comes into contact. And this helps to create another level of tension, instability, and contradiction within and between the moral orders that animate human social life.

The third reason for the imperfect correspondence between institutional and socialized moral order brings us back to our model of human personhood. At issue is more than simply the intrinsic limits or multiplicity of moral orders as cultural entities. Again, human motivation, action, and personhood themselves matter here. Part of the reason why the moral orders internalized "inside" of people do not entirely match the moral orders constituting and embedded in the institutions outside of and encompassing those people is that animals that are moral and believing actively participate in their own socialization, as discriminating agents who judge, embrace, reject, and modify. The consciousness and self-consciousness that place moral belief at the center of human action also give rise to capacities for human creativity and discrimination that help to constitute human persons as active subjects with agency. As self-conscious animals, humans are able to "step back" from and develop alternative and creative perspectives on moral orders and institutions, even those that beget and envelop their very own lives. To do otherwise would be less than human. As moral agents, humans are able and often compelled to consider, to evaluate, to judge the goodness, truth, and rightness of the moral orders they are taught by socializers to subjectively embrace. To do otherwise would again be less than human. The very "nature" of human personhood modeled here, therefore, explains why people are never mere "cultural dopes," why socialization is never entirely effective or complete, and why humanly intended social change can and does happen. *For moral and believing animals are also necessarily* creative *and discriminating animals who find themselves with sufficient (but not absolute) "distance" in consciousness from both their own selves and from that around them which is not their selves, to be able to exercise their wills in the making*

17. Robert Bellah, Richard Madsen, William Sullivan, Ann Swidler, and Steven Tipton, *Habits of the Heart* (Berkeley: University of California Press, 1985).

of meaningful, if constrained, choices about the moral order or orders to which they will commit their lives—that is to say, choices about who they will become and therefore how they will spend their lives. Something like this is what provides the basis for believing in the moral responsibility of sentient human persons that is essential to successful humanistic (if not all) legal and social systems.

Notice, however, that in this model, no human ever entirely transcends or successfully "digs below" the particularistic, historical narratives and traditions that comprise any moral order, in order to arrive at either an objective "view from nowhere" or some indubitable, universal foundation of knowledge and judgment. That impossible Enlightenment aspiration, we increasingly realize, was in many cases a self-deceived conceit of some self-divinizing intellectuals inebriated with their belief of having finally thrown God out of the universe. In fact, all any human person has ever had or has to work from are the materials of the historically relative, particular narratives and traditions available to him or her in his or her place on earth and in history. However, human persons also normally have some capacity to gain some critical distance and comparative perspective—even while always operating within the limits of available moral orders—which creates some degree of decision, of creativity, of agency in the formation of the self in relation to moral order. And it is this that keeps people from being cultural dopes, from perfectly internalizing through socialization the external system, from always only reproducing the existing social order.

There is of course much more that might be said about moral orders and people's relations to them. A more fully developed account, for one thing, would further elaborate on the troubled, conflicted, and rebellious human impulses toward moral order. Human life is not a simple story of smooth and happy fulfillment of moral imperatives. People often struggle mightily at different levels to come to grips with the moral orders they inhabit and enact. There is in human life, besides our profound dependence on and enthusiasm for moral order, a simultaneous element of chronic discontent with moral order, of sometimes desperate impulses to resist and escape it. The best of saints as well as sinners can live bedeviled and anguished lives, in part because of the sometimes torturous pressures and complicated obligations that our inescapable moral condition generates. No doubt the life of the subconscious plays an important role in much of this struggle, resistance, and agony as well.

A more fully developed account would also need to elaborate on the realities of power and social conflict, which normative theories of culture have often been criticized for neglecting. The moral order perspective suggested in these pages can ably comprehend and explain power and social conflict. Moral orders empower. They generate and organize resources and agency for accomplishing their aims. Moral orders also make contending claims against rivals that structure and mobilize social division and conflict. The very creation of difference, valuation, and judgment at the heart of moral ordering not only provides meaning and direction to human existence, but also is precisely that which generates and sustains the distinctions, hierarchies, and inequalities that pervade human social life. Thus any analysis of social stratification or oppression can and finally must reference the thickly moral character of human persons and social structures as described in these pages. All of these are issues and dynamics that continued scholarship pursuing the "moral, believing animals" perspective described here will need more fully to explore and develop.

The approach offered in the previous pages helps us to avoid a number of besetting missteps in cultural theory. It enables us to speak of internally motivated, purposive human action without falling into the over-simplifications inherent in the Parsonian view of culture as instilling in actors the ends of action. It justifies our taking a strong position on the power and importance of socialization in social reproduction, without conceiving of those socialized as passive recipients of cultural norms, values, and ends—since they are always both the objects and subjects of their own socialization. It allows us to think about society as truly having an ordered cultural system, without supposing that such a system is unified, consensual, well bounded, and always integrating. The model of human personhood and culture outlined here also enables us to recognize and analyze the externally constraining influence of culture, without losing sight of the simultaneous internally motivating dimension of culture. Moreover, this model conceives of culture in a way that allows it both to provide instrumental tools for accomplishing purposive ends and to define purposes of human action themselves in relation to the right, true, and good of a moral order or orders. Such a model likewise allows us to speak of the ("habitus"-like)[18] subconscious, unintentional, and institutional-practice aspects of culture's role in social reproduction, without losing the creative and purposive dimensions of reproduction and transformation as well. Finally, the model described here provides an account for notions of human freedom and responsibility that does not lapse into liberal (e.g., Rawlsian) political theory's make-believe notions of individual autonomy and self-determined moral agency.

And finally, what of rational self-interest? Any social theory that fails to account for the reality of human self-centeredness and self-regarding choice-making will not get far. Most, if not arguably all, people turn out to have a propensity toward self-centeredness and often subtle and overt tendencies toward sheer selfishness, far exceeding what many optimistic, modern views of humanity are comfortable admitting. And this endemic human self-centeredness manifests itself pervasively in social life, a reality for which social theory has to account. Nevertheless, it is helpful to register a few points here that might shape our theorizing on this matter.

First, it is not obvious that human selfishness is conceptually identical to the rational pursuit of self-interest. Being a selfishly oriented person does not automatically make one an economics textbook model of the rationally calculating, strategic, ends-oriented, maximizing actor. There are many ways to live a self-centered life, not all of which embody *Homo economicus*. Second, even if human self-centeredness is pervasive and powerful, that does not automatically mean that self-interest is the only or even central motive for human action. People may and, I suggest, normally do act based on a variety of competing and complementary motives, not all of which are reducible to strict self-interest.[19] For this reason, very often people's self-interests (at least understood in terms that make reasonable sense to think of them that way) are often overridden by moti-

18. Pierre Bourdieu, *Outline of a Theory of Practice* (Cambridge: Cambridge University Press, 1977).

19. Amitai Etzioni, for example, has proposed a "bi-utility" approach to motivation in *The Moral Dimension;* also see Christian Smith, *Resisting Reagan* (Chicago: University of Chicago Press, 1996), 190–98; Manstead, "The Role of Moral Norm in the Attitude-Behavior Relation"; Michael Wallach and Lise Wallach, *Psychology's Sanction for Selfishness: The Error of Egoism in Theory and Therapy* (San Francisco: W. H. Freeman, 1983).

vations springing from their moral commitments that are irreducible to self-interest. This is not to suggest that the world is populated by saints and angels, simply that even the kind of animals humans actually *are* turn out simply not always to act entirely or perhaps even primarily according to self-interested motives. Which is a good thing for us all, in the long run.

Third, there are very few, if any, culturally unmediated human interests, at least of the sort that proximately motivate action. What may be in the interest of a human self is rarely if ever a fixed, predetermined, common entity. Rather, interests are powerfully constituted, bounded, and directed by larger moral orders. Thus we humans may have fundamental interests in, say, individual and kin survival and enjoying physical and psychological pleasures. But these hardly tell us much specific about how to live our lives, any more than the physiological need to eat determines whether what you will have for dinner tonight will include steak, snake, bean sprouts, rotted fish (a delicacy in ancient Rome), or deep-fried, live baby chicks (a delicacy in parts of China). By the time elemental human interests get worked out in actual, lived human action, they have inevitably and thoroughly been defined, interpreted, and guided by culturally specific normative categories and directives. Thus "self-interest" can hardly explain human action apart from the thick moral orders of the cultural realm that mediate them and so hardly provides an adequate keystone on which to rest social theory. Rather, it is moral order that merits our greatest theoretical and analytical attention.

Finally, to the extent that people today actually do act clearly in the pursuit of rational self-interest, they do so much less as a reflection of some innate, natural impulse and much more in conformity with a socially and historically particular moral order that tells them that the way they *should* act is precisely in a rationally self-interested manner. Rational self-interest ultimately does have moorings in some elemental features of the human condition. But to get from them to consistent, rationally self-interested action in observable, everyday life involves heavy doses of socialization into the moral orders of market capitalism, liberal democracy, and Western individualism. Thus most of what any of us commonly conduct or witness as rationally self-interested behavior is itself largely following the dictates of the particular moral order that we just so happen to usually take for granted as natural, even though it is in fact constructed and particular. In which case, rational choice theory does not trump a normative theory of culture by reducing and reinterpreting the variety and complexity of human motivations into the singular motive of rational self-interest. Rather, if anything, a normative or moral theory of culture, such as the one suggested here, reinterprets rational choice theory as describing one particular mode of human motivation and action that reflects and embodies a specific moral order situated in a particular place in history and culture.

Addendum: Why Are Humans Moral Animals?

Why are humans apparently unique among all animals in being profoundly moral animals? It may be impossible to answer this question definitively, but it is worth considering. Some people will say that humans are uniquely moral animals because they are made "in the image" of a personal, moral God, who created them uniquely to reflect, know, and obey God. Other people will say that humans are moral because of the relatively large brains our species acquired through evolutionary development, which are neurologically capable of depths and complexities of evaluation and emotion unavailable to smaller brained animals. Maybe one or the other of these accounts is right, or maybe both are right.

Yet another account of human morality that does *not* seem to work, however, is the sociobiological (and, more recently, evolutionary psychology) explanation claiming that humans are moral because being so has had the effect of increasing their reproductive fitness. In this view, those protohumans that possessed a genetic disposition toward moral action, or that by chance learned to act morally, proved more fit in survival and natural selection. Such morality is said to have promoted the kind of cooperation and functional self-sacrifice that, in certain situations, may have increased the protohuman's capacity, or perhaps that of his or her kin or tribe, to survive. The gene pools of those with moral propensities prevailed, then, while those without died off, leaving the descendants of the more fit (us) with selected-on "moral genes" that now govern our consciousness and behavior. Thus "the perception that morality exists is an epigenetic manifestation of our genes, which so manipulate humans as to make them believe that some behaviors are morally 'good' so that people behave in ways that are good for their genes."[20]

But sociobiological and evolutionary psychology accounts are beset with a number of significant—and, in my view, fatal—problems. This essay can obviously only begin to suggest sociobiology and evolutionary psychology's problems and casts a vote more than it offers a definitive critique, toward which many others have already contributed.[21] First, such explanations invariably reduce the rich and complex character of human morality to the single dimension of "altruism." What they mean by altruism is something like "any act that increases the reproductive potential of another organism relative to the actor's own potential." This flattens and distorts the multidimensional reality of morality discussed in this essay, leaving as a remainder an emaciated concept. Indeed, by sociobiologists' own admission, this definition would allow that having a genetic predisposition to have bad teeth would be altruistic, since that would cause that organism to eat less food, leaving more food for others to consume. This

20. Francisco Ayala, "Human Nature: One Evolutionist's View," in Warren Brown, Nancey Murphy, and H. Newton Malony (eds.), *Whatever Happened to the Soul?* (Minneapolis: Fortress Press, 1998), 47. For some major works in sociobiology, see Edward O. Wilson, *Sociobiology* (Cambridge: Harvard University Press, 1975); Wilson, *On Human Nature* (Cambridge: Harvard University Press, 1978); Richard Dawkins, *The Selfish Gene* (Oxford: Oxford University Press, 1976); David Barasch, *The Whisperings Within* (New York: Harper and Row, 1979); Henry Plotkin, *Evolution in Mind: An Introduction to Evolutionary Psychology* (Cambridge: Harvard University Press, 1998); Robert Wright, *The Moral Animal: Evolutionary Psychology and Everyday Life* (New York: Pantheon, 1994); David Buss, *Evolutionary Psychology: The New Science of the Mind* (Boston: Allyn and Bacon, 1999).

21. See, for example, Philip Kitcher, *Vaulting Ambition: Sociobiology and the Quest for Human Nature* (Cambridge: MIT Press, 1985); Hilary Rose and Steven Rose, *Alas, Poor Darwin: Arguments against Evolutionary Psychology* (New York: Harmony Books, 2000); Marshall Sahlins, *The Uses and Abuses of Biology* (Ann Arbor: University of Michigan Press, 1976); Stephen Jay Gould and Richard Lewontin, "The Spandrels of San Marco and the Panglossian Paradigm: A Critique of the Adaptationist Programme," *Proceedings of the Royal Society*, vol. B205 (1979): 581–98; Barry Schwartz, *The Battle for Human Nature: Science, Morality, and Modern Life* (New York: W. W. Norton, 1986).

points out the problem, among many others, that the logic of sociobiology and evolutionary psychology lacks an adequate appreciation for conscious human intentions in moral action.[22]

But even if we grant its shriveled image of morality, the sociobiological and evolutionary psychology account has difficulty explaining the many empirical cases of altruism to non-kin. If sacrificing oneself for the welfare of others consistently increased one's own reproductive fitness, then sociobiology's account would work. But self-sacrifice normally decreases one's reproductive fitness, lessening, in small and sometimes big ways, the chances of survival. Sociobiologists have therefore answered that problem by introducing the idea of "inclusive fitness."[23] Their proposal is essentially that—since the true "actors" in this process are "selfish genes" and not the organisms that carry them—what really matters is the survival of one's genetic material, which one shares in various proportions with one's kin, more than one's own bodily self as a living organism. So, just as a honeybee may help ensure the survival of its own genetic material shared by other bees in its hive by sacrificing its life to sting an intruder, so a human mother may help ensure the survival of her own genetic material by sacrificing herself to save her children from death or danger (or, more precisely, the mother's genes compel the organism of the mother to sacrifice itself to save the organisms of her children, in order to ensure the survival of the same genes, one-half of which are also carried by the children's organisms). Thus is the reproductive fitness of selfish genes increased by altruism—when fitness is inclusive of all carriers of one's shared genes. As leading sociobiologist Edward O. Wilson has put it, "The individual pays, his genes and tribe gain, altruism spreads."[24] But if this were so, then people would only be altruistic to those who share their genes, and only in rough proportion to the extent that they do share their genes— children would elicit more altruism than, say, nieces and nephews. But that is very often not the case. People frequently do sacrifice themselves

22. C. Daniel Batson, "Sociobiology and the Role of Religion in Promoting Prosocial Behavior: An Alternative View," *Journal of Personality and Social Psychology* 45, no. 6 (1983): 1383.

23. W. D. Hamilton, *Narrow Roads of Gene Land* (New York: Freeman, 1996).

24. Edward O. Wilson, "The Biological Basis of Morality," *Atlantic Monthly*, April 1998, 65.

in various ways for people who do not share their genes, even sometimes for foreigners and strangers.[25] Indeed, some moral systems that billions of people embrace command people to love their neighbors as themselves, to love their enemies, to repay evil with good, and to perform many actions that normally reduce reproductive fitness. "Inclusive fitness" therefore does not in the end explain the oddity of selfish genes acting altruistically. Morality is often not functional for survival, yet people act morally anyway.

The sociobiological and evolutionary psychology explanation of morality also has difficulty making a plausible jump from the (anthropomorphized) gene as self-interested actor to the conscious and self-conscious person acting with moral intentions. Somewhere in the process, the alleged genes have to trick or manipulate the thinking person into purposive beliefs and acts that may not be good for the person but are good for the genes. Sociobiologists and evolutionary psychologists have introduced revisionist notions such as "empathetic emotions," "reciprocal altruism," and "religious kinship imagery" to help make this leap.[26] But these moves inevitably shift explanatory weight from hard-wired genetic self-interest to human agents as perceiving, feeling, discerning, evaluating, choosing actors—in short, toward human freedom and responsibility. The choice in the end is between a model of humans as genetic dopes who are consistently hoodwinked by their genetics to sacrifice themselves naively for the sake of their selfish genes; or a model of humans as possessing some strong genetic propensities toward altruism that are significantly mediated by supragenetic capacities for understanding, awareness, commitment, and choice. Choosing the first model eliminates any shred of our belief in human freedom, dignity, choice, rights, and responsibility— which is to say, morality itself as we know it. But choosing the second model—something like which I hope is the more obviously preferable

25. Smith, *Resisting Reagan*.

26. M. L. Hoffman. "Is Altruism Part of Human Nature?" *Journal of Personality and Social Psychology* 40 (1981): 121–37; Batson, "Sociobiology and the Role of Religion in Promoting Prosocial Behavior"; Schwartz, *The Battle for Human Nature;* Doug Jones, "Evolutionary Psychology," *Annual Review of Anthropology* 28 (1999): 553–75.

option between the two—automatically opens up new theoretical explanatory possibilities that no longer particularly need sociobiological assumptions as starting points. In short, sociobiological and evolutionary
psychology accounts of human morality either entail a radical reductionism that is intellectually problematic and, for most of us, morally objectionable; or they require supplemental theoretical elaborations that tend
to undermine the need for sociobiological assumptions and logic in the
first place.[27]

Sociobiology and evolutionary psychology's particular moral problems
may be worth developing a bit, just to be clear about them. When human
morality is redefined entirely in relation to reproductive fitness—so that
morality is no longer driven by natural law or the will of God or self-
evident inherent moral values—then we lose any real moral standard by
which to judge actions. Genetic survival and extinction in a competitive
environment is all that is. Beyond that we can have nothing evaluative to
say about which genes successfully reproduce or how they do it. Indeed,
we no longer even possess standards for value judgments about what
constitutes progress in evolution. It is finally of no more value that humans survive than do bacteria. Why, on sociobiological grounds, should
one be any "better" than another?[28] Furthermore, if some humans have
genetic propensities that enable them to survive and thrive while, or even
because, other humans die out, it is difficult, given the sociobiological
account, to explain why that should not happen; or why, if it did, anyone
should necessarily feel any moral concern or sense of tragedy about it.
Some die. Some live. Natural processes work their way out. That is all. If
any sociobiology or evolutionary psychology worth considering theoretically gives us any reliable normative direction, it is that the fittest genes
should survive and the organisms that carry them should do what they
need to do to ensure that outcome. Even then, any notion of "should"
makes little sense, really, since what will happen will simply happen by

27. For an excellent discussion of related matters, see John Dupré, *Human
Nature and the Limits of Science* (New York: Oxford University Press, 2001).

28. Francisco Ayala, "The Evolutionary Concepts of Progress," in G. A. Almond et al. (eds.), *Progress and Its Discontents* (Berkeley: University of California
Press, 1982).

natural process. For sociobiology and evolutionary psychology to end up with any serious substantive morality requires smuggling in auxiliary assumptions and commitments that are alien to its own intellectual system.

Thus, while ideas like "inclusive fitness" may explain certain actions between specific individuals in particular circumstances, they hardly account for the kind of ever-present orientation to moral order that saturates and governs all of human social action and interaction that this chapter describes. Sociobiology and evolutionary psychology inevitably explain morality in functional terms, but morality is not always, perhaps even often, functional in ways that matter to sociobiology and evolutionary psychology. Their accounts of human morality are thus not particularly plausible. They often read like nervous attempts by apostles of the Darwinian evolutionary paradigm to salvage the paradigm from the very uncomfortable, ubiquitous anomalies of human moral order and action as we humans experience and observe them. Edward O. Wilson's recent popular restatement of the sociobiological account of morality, for instance, is so governed by a naive and un-self-reflexive faith in scientific objectivity and authority and so replete with false dichotomies, gross generalizations, simplistic reductionisms, and ill-informed conflations of religious differences that it is a marvel that critical thinkers take these kinds of sociobiological explanations of morality seriously, even though they do emanate from the Ivy League.[29] Sociobiology and evolutionary psychology's case might be merely amusing, were it not for the monumentally misanthropic practical consequences that should follow any widespread embrace of its program. One can only hope that most moral, believing animals have more sense than to let that happen.[30]

Rejecting the reductionism of explaining human morality as serving the interests of selfish genes, however, does not require the dismissal of an interest in biological factors in human social life. Nor does it necessitate the rejection of possible evolutionary frameworks of explanation. In whatever other ways that human animals may be mental or moral or spiritual beings, we are also clearly biological organisms, and there is no reason to

---

29. See Wilson, "Biological Basis of Morality."

30. See Wendell Berry, *Life Is a Miracle: An Essay against Modern Superstition* (Washington, D.C.: Counterpoint, 2000).

think that biology and mental, moral, and spiritual life do not interact. Of course they do.

A much more plausible account of human morality than that offered by traditional sociobiology and more recent evolutionary psychology requires an appreciation for the multileveled character of life and the world, and for the reality of emergent properties. Such an approach is self-consciously antireductionistic and attracted to the ideas of emergence and supervenience. This is not the place to elaborate these concepts.[31] Suffice it to say here that more plausible accounts of the sources of human morality suggest that human biology gives rise to the conditions necessary for the existence and operation of morality in human life—even if morality itself does not directly serve some biological survival function. Whether as the result of long evolutionary development or having been created this way by a divine Creator, or both, human animals have the biological infrastructure that makes them capable of the kind of intellectual and emotional work necessary to live and act as moral animals.

The biologist Francisco Ayala suggests three necessary and jointly sufficient, biologically grounded, cognitive conditions for the emergence of human morality: first, the ability to anticipate the consequences of one's actions; second, the ability to make value judgments ("to perceive certain objects or deeds as more desirable than others"); and third, the ability to choose between alternative courses of action. According to Ayala,

> ethical behavior is an attribute of the biological makeup of humans and is, in that sense, a product of biological evolution. But I see no evidence that ethical behavior *developed* because it was adaptive in itself. I find it hard to see how *evaluating* certain actions as either good or evil (not just choosing some action rather than others, or evaluating them with respect to their practical consequences) would promote the reproductive fitness of the eval-

31. But some helpful starting points include Donald Polkinghorne, *Narrative Knowing and the Human Sciences* (Albany: State University of New York Press, 1988); Nancey Murphey and George Ellis, *On the Moral Nature of the Universe* (Minneapolis: Fortress Press, 1996); Nancey Murphey, *Anglo-American Postmodernity: Philosophical Perspectives on Science, Religion, and Ethics* (Boulder, Colo.: Westview Press, 1997), particularly the chapter titled "Supervenience and the Nonreducibility of Ethics to Biology."

uators. Nor do I see how there might be some form of "incipient" ethical behavior that would then be further promoted by natural selection. The three necessary conditions for there being ethical behavior are manifestations of advanced intellectual abilities. It seems . . . that the likely target of natural selection was the development of these advanced intellectual capacities. . . . We make moral judgements as a consequence of our eminent intellectual abilities, not as an innate way for achieving biological gain.[32]

This argument makes sense and is helpful as far as it goes. Even so, Ayala's case only explains the biologically grounded conditions necessary for the emergence of morality. It does not explain why those conditions did in fact give rise to morality. Animals with the intellectual capacity to anticipate consequences of action, to make value judgments, and to choose among alternatives could very well put those capacities only to instrumentally functional uses. Intellectually endowed protohumans, for instance, might see that sharper spear heads make hunting easier, may judge that easier hunting is more desirable than more difficult hunting, and so may choose to invest time and effort into fashioning pointed spear heads. But why should such animals go beyond putting their eminent intellectual capacities to instrumentally functional purposes, adding to that the engagement in distinctively moral purposes? Why start making the very different sort of claims that some things are not only desirable but good, right, just, worthy, and noble in and of themselves, independent of their instrumental function?

The slippage in Ayala's argument is found in his second condition, the "ability to make value judgments." For there is a crucial difference between desirable and morally right. Ayala does note that moral judgments are a particular subclass of value judgment, those that "are not dictated by one's own interest or profit but by regard for others, . . . [that] concern the values of right and wrong in human conduct." But in his discussion, Ayala only speaks about the conditions that make morality possible, not those that have made it actual. But that is inadequate. Just because I have the capacity to become a skydiver does not mean that I have or ever will. I won't. Why then *are* human animals such profoundly morally oriented and guided beings? Why do they, for instance, recurrently seek truth for its own sake, and carry out moral obligations even sometimes at great

32. Ayala, "Human Nature."

cost to themselves? Ayala's argument does not really explain the motivation or mechanism. He does provide a smart and helpful critique of traditional sociobiological accounts of human morality, and he takes helpful steps in thinking well about the relationship between biology and morality. But he stops short of offering a complete argument about human morality's sources.

The British philosopher Anthony O'Hear has recently advanced what may be a helpful contribution to this question in his book *Beyond Evolution: Human Nature and the Limits of Evolutionary Explanation.*[33] O'Hear focuses on the particular human cognitive trait of being not only conscious but also self-conscious creatures. In self-consciousness, O'Hear finds the source of reflective questioning about the reasons for assertions and beliefs, the testing of claims and convictions in light of what is really true and good, the understanding of life in moral terms. The argument runs as follows. Merely conscious animals experience pleasures, pains, and needs and react to the world in terms of them. Conscious animals may have dispositions and even beliefs, may accumulate knowledge about their environment, may engage in various practices, and can actively respond to life in the world. But humans are not merely conscious animals, they are also *self-conscious* animals. And self-conscious animals not only have experiences, pleasures, pains, and beliefs but are aware that they have them. The self-conscious animal *knows that it is a knower.* It is thus able as a self to "step back from" its experiences, knowledge, beliefs, and reactions and consider them from different points of view. Self-consciousness thus introduces a new dimension of awareness that creates various forms of "distance" between the self and the thoughts and experiences and desires of the self, which the merely conscious creature cannot. And it is this distance that introduces the "strong evaluations" entailed in morality. For the self-conscious self, now able to distance itself from its own thoughts, beliefs, desires, and reactions, naturally and inevitably comes to consider the possibility that its thoughts and beliefs and desires and reactions are neither necessarily shared by others nor the only ones

33. Anthony O'Hear, *Beyond Evolution: Human Nature and the Limits of Evolutionary Explanation* (Oxford: Oxford University Press, 1997). Pages 1–30 are particularly relevant for the following discussion. Also see Kelly Nicholson, *Body and Soul: The Transcendence of Materialism* (Boulder, Colo.: Westview Press, 1997).

it might hold or choose or feel. Thus the thoughts, beliefs, desires, and reactions of self-conscious selves are not simply experienced in stream-of-consciousness but become distinct *objects* capable of more or less detached examination and evaluation. This gives rise to the search for standards more objective or reliable than the self's own thoughts, feelings, desires, and reactions by which to evaluate their merits. In this way, I realize that my beliefs and dispositions are, as O'Hear puts it,

> just that—mine; and that being mine, they are not necessarily in tune with those of others or with the world. In other words, they are not necessarily true or correct; but are but one route through the world apart from me. Once the soul becomes aware of the nature and condition of its own knowledge and dispositions, it is led to postulate an absolute standard against which its mental map is to be judged. And so we get an aspect of reason and reasoning quite different from [Humean] . . . conceptions of reason as the instrument and slave of life. Its nature is also to be the critic of life and the passions.[34]

This then is the primal spring of morality, as O'Hear explains: "At any moment the demands of life's flow can be held up by us to scrutiny, we can step outside the steady stream of judgements and practical decisions we are continually making so as to see if they satisfy some standard not limited by the limits of our life or cognitive powers. We can, as it were, step outside our cognitive and practical frameworks and question the validity of the frameworks themselves."

The reason, by this account, that humans are peculiar among animals in being moral animals is that humans are uniquely self-conscious animals. Self-consciousness gives rise to reflective distances between the self and its cognitions, emotions, and desires. And those distances provoke the quest for standards above and beyond the self's cognitions, emotions, and desires by which they might be evaluated as worthy of thinking, feeling, and believing or not. O'Hear writes: "The very fact of being self-conscious about our beliefs, of being in the full sense believers . . . initiates a process in which we search for what is true because it is true, rather than because it serves some interest of ours." One assumption undergirding O'Hear's argument that is not very obviously said is that humans

---

34. O'Hear, *Beyond Evolution*, 24. The following quotes come from pp. 24–25, 30.

normally seek to bring their thoughts, feelings, beliefs, and desires into line with those that they should objectively think, feel, believe, and want; for, as he puts it, "we cannot at the one time believe something and doubt its truth."[35] It is thus the identification and formulation of those more objective standards that create the basis for and content of the moral orders that humans produce, inhabit, discharge, and defend.

Whatever else are the strengths and weaknesses of O'Hear's argument, he has at least provided an account of the sources of human morality that does not appear to suffer from the functionalism of sociobiology, evolutionary psychology, and other social utility theories. Humans are moral animals not primarily because morality serves some instrumental interest (even if in cases it may). Humans are moral animals, rather, because they experience, in part as a result of their self-consciousness, a particular relationship to themselves and the world that evokes a search for standards beyond themselves by which they may evaluate themselves. This is an account of morality that also takes human cognizance and intention seriously, as the sociobiological account does not. On these two counts, it is commendable. Whether or not we can press the discussion further to a more satisfying explanation, including one concerning the sources of self-consciousness, remains to be seen.

In any case, what is clear for my purposes is that, whether we are able to explain morality's sources well or not, human animals are in fact profoundly and nearly inescapably moral and believing animals. And until we accept and account for that fact, our theories of culture and action will be badly deficient. It will be the task of the following chapters to elaborate and support that claim.

---

35. O'Hear, *Beyond Evolution*, 30. This cognitive antidissonance assumption is not an unreasonable one, although it is one that some may contest.

THREE

BELIEVING ANIMALS

For centuries, many Western thinkers have tried to identify a universal and certain foundation for human knowledge. Various movements within the eighteenth- and nineteenth-century "Enlightenment" in particular sought to specify an authoritative foundation of knowledge not based on the revelation, faith, and tradition of Christianity.[1] Instead this project sought to identify a strong foundation for knowledge that would be secular (nontheistic), universal (applicable to all people despite their differences), and indubitable (irrefutable and certain). One way to understand philosophical epistemology since René Descartes is as a story of repeated unsuccessful attempts to identify this kind of foundation of human knowledge. Like the would-be champions who sought to become the one able to draw the fabled sword from the stone and so become king, many philosophers have ventured to identify this prized strong foundation of knowledge on which the rational, universal, modern social order could be built. In each case, however, other philosophers always stepped forward to demonstrate why their attempts at this secular, universal, indubitable epistemology did not work.

---

1. James Byrne, *Religion and the Enlightenment* (Louisville: Westminster John Knox, 1996); Dorinda Outram, *The Enlightenment* (Cambridge: Cambridge University Press, 1995).

45

As a consequence, what we have come rather decisively to see in recent decades is that this epistemological project itself is fatally flawed and that all such attempts to discover a universal, indubitable foundation of knowledge have failed and necessarily will fail. Strong foundationalism is dead. Its quest has come up empty-handed. The sword remains fast in the stone without a champion to remove it. There *is* no secular, universal, indubitable foundation of knowledge available to us humans.[2]

Homo Credens

What we have come to see is that, at bottom, *we are all really believers.* The lives that we live and the knowledge we possess are based crucially on sets of basic assumptions and beliefs, about which three characteristics deserve note. First, our elemental assumptions and beliefs themselves cannot be empirically verified or established with certainty. They are starting points, trusted premises, postulated axioms, presuppositions—"below" which there is no deeper or more final justification, proof, or verification establishing them. In philosophical terms, these beliefs and commitments may be "justified," but they are not "justifiable."[3] Rather, they themselves provide the suppositional grounds on which any sense of justification, proof, or verification for a given knowledge system are built.[4]

2. The literature on this point is immense, but key works include Alasdair MacIntyre, *Three Rival Versions of Moral Enquiry* (Notre Dame, Ind.: University of Notre Dame Press, 1988); Nicholas Wolterstorff, *Reason within the Bounds of Religion* (Grand Rapids: Eerdmans, 1976); Richard Rorty, *Philosophy and the Mirror of Nature* (Princeton, N.J.: Princeton University Press, 1979).

3. See, for example, Alvin Plantinga, *Warrant and Proper Function* (Oxford: Oxford University Press, 1993). For a similar idea stated in other terms, see Michael Polanyi, *Personal Knowledge* (Chicago: University of Chicago Press, 1958); also see Polanyi, *Science, Faith, and Society* (London: Oxford University Press, 1948); Polanyi, *The Tacit Dimension* (Garden City, N.Y.: Doubleday, 1983).

4. Two relevant, important, and illuminating books on this point are William Alston, *The Reliability of Sense Perception* (Ithaca, N.Y.: Cornell University Press, 1993), which exposes the fatal epistemic circularity of arguments that human sense perceptual faculties are reliable; and C. A. J. Coady, *Testimony: A Philosophical*

At a very basic level, for instance, it is safe to guess that probably most readers of this essay believe in causation (that forces and agents can cause effects in or on others), in natural regularity (that the natural world as we observe it works the same way in places where we do not observe it), and in the temporal continuity of experience (that life when we wake up tomorrow will function very similarly to the way it functions today). These we believe in so "deeply" that we do not even think about them. We simply assume them and build up the living of our lives on them. None of those beliefs, however, can be verified as definitely true in fact. There is simply nothing that could do so. All we can do is assume them in faith, and then presumably find them to be sufficiently trustworthy and functional assumptions to live by.[5] In principle there is nothing that must stop a person from being an unbeliever with regard to these assumptions. I could live my life in full expectation that some unknown impending morning when I wake up everything will be radically different. And in fact a day *could very well* come when my personal unbelief in the temporal continuity of experience is fully validated— none of us can know that this could never happen. (Indeed, the many Christians who believe in the second coming of Christ as consummating the "last days" with Jesus descending on the clouds do sincerely believe in something quite like this.) Thus we all proceed with whatever assumed basic beliefs we trust in and build our lives on, even though we cannot finally know them to be right.

Study (New York: Oxford University Press, 1992), which demonstrates our inescapable reliance on the unverifiable testimony of others.

5. A key motif in many popular fictional narratives is the "pulling the rug out from under" key characters' fundamentally assumed worlds, with the effect of radically undermining their (and perhaps the reader's or viewer's) elementally assumed realities. This, for instance, has been the appeal of television shows like *The Twilight Zone* and *The X-Files*. It is the fundamental plot of numerous popular movies, as with the 1998 film *The Truman Show* and the 1999 box office hit *The Matrix*. J. K. Rowling achieved an analogous effect with a key character in the climax of her 2000 best-seller, *Harry Potter and the Goblet of Fire*. C. S. Lewis's *Out of the Silent Planet* likewise turns the universe inside-out by showing our earth actually to be "Malacandra," not an island home of life and communication in an otherwise empty universe, but—from the living, dancing universe's point of view—an isolated center of silence and dark mystery.

To conclude this first point: Some people do or have believed that humans are born to be free, while others have believed that some humans are born to be slaves. Some believe that men and women are equal, while others that women are essentially the lesser of the two. Some people believe that a Great Spirit created the world long ago, while others believe the universe is the result of a naturalistic Big Bang long ago. Some believe that a natural law infuses life and the world, while others believe that morality and regularity are social constructions of relative human invention. Who is right and who is wrong? Disagreement does not mean that all are wrong or that all is relative. Some of these beliefs might be right. Indeed, we ourselves believe some of them are right. But our convictions and disagreements about these are based precisely on larger systems of beliefs grounded in deeper suppositional beliefs, and we cannot get around the fact that these starting-point assumptions and beliefs cannot be empirically verified or established with certainty. We simply cannot set aside our basic belief commitments and find independent evidence definitively to demonstrate that one or another of these beliefs is true. At bottom, we simply believe them or we don't, for what we take to be arguably more or less good reasons.

A second important characteristic of our presuppositional assumptions, implicit in the previous discussion but that I should make explicit, is that most of these starting-point assumptions and beliefs are not universal. By "universal" here, I mean simply the descriptive point of a belief or assumption being found everywhere among humans, and I note empirically that human assumptions and beliefs in fact are not.[6] They are thus neither intellectually self-evident to nor actually shared by the rest of the human race.[7] It is true that, for any one person to assume and believe some

6. In another sense, not meant here, "universal" can mean a belief or assumption itself claiming that it is applicable or true everywhere and always. Thus people can hold beliefs, such as that humans possess inalienable rights or that Jesus Christ is Lord of all, that they understand as being applicable everywhere, even though they are not empirically found everywhere among humans.

7. For my purposes, I am content to make this point as worded, recognizing the possibility, as some philosophers argue, that certain few basic beliefs—such as that there exist external objects—are and must be universally taken for granted, Thomas Reid's notion of common sense and Ludwig Wittgenstein's discussion of

assumptions and beliefs means that some larger cultural community of which they are a part, some historical tradition, some "web of inter-locutors"[8] shares these assumptions and beliefs together. For sustaining such sets of assumptions and beliefs requires a community, a "plausibility structure" to suppose, affirm, and communicate them.[9] Lone individuals who maintain idiosyncratic assumptions and beliefs about elemental reality that are not shared by others are people we normally take to be mentally ill.

Nevertheless, a community of belief does not universality make. All around the world and across history, different believing communities have supposed as starting points very different, often incompatible sets of assumptions and beliefs. One good introductory course in anthropology and one in world history should be enough to make that perfectly clear. Some societies believe identities and worth must be achieved, while others mark them as ascribed from birth. Some peoples embrace cultures that deeply prize the violence of warfare and conquest, while others live within cultural worlds of peace and cooperation. Some communities ground institutional legitimacy in rational legal authority, while others in charisma or tradition. Some cultures venerate their elderly as wise and honorable, while others cherish youth and view their elderly as insignificant annoyances. Some peoples believe that land, beaches, and water can and should be privately owned, while others have been no more able to conceive of the private ownership of land than the private ownership of air, the sky, and the stars. Some cultures believe that intimate and enduring marriage partner relationships should be formed entirely on considerations of economic and political interests determined by family elders, while others believe that the selection of a marriage mate is rightly each individual's personal choice to be determined by his or her own subjective experience of romantic love. Such examples can be vastly multiplied. But the basic

---

shared world pictures being cases in point. See Nicholas Wolterstorff, *Thomas Reid and the Story of Epistemology* (Cambridge: Cambridge University Press, 2001), 215–49; also see John Searle, *The Construction of Social Reality* (New York: Free Press, 1995).

8. Charles Taylor, *Sources of the Self* (Cambridge: Harvard University Press, 1989), 36.

9. Peter Berger, *The Sacred Canopy* (New York: Doubleday, 1967).

point concerns the nonuniversality of presuppositional beliefs and assumptions that constitute believing communities' elemental "cultural ontologies."[10]

We would be mistaken here to suppose—following the often misleading "traditional" versus "modern" society dichotomy that appeals, for different reasons, to both romantics and liberals—that primordial, world-defining beliefs shape the mythical worlds of primitives but not of enlightened moderns. We moderns are in our own peculiar ways no less deeply trusting in unverifiable objects of belief and faith than any premoderns have ever been. The Aztecs willingly engaged in the human sacrifice of many thousands of their own people every year on the alter of the sun god Tenochtitlan, believing that the victims' blood contained an energy needed to nourish the gods and the universe. Contemporary Americans willingly sacrifice about five thousand of our teenagers every year in large steel boxes propelled rapidly through space, because, finally, we believe in the reality and moral worth of individual freedom, mobility, and self-direction. Certain ancient Hebrews believed that God spoke to them in dreams and through angels—indeed, they experienced it and recorded it in writing. Certain contemporary Americans believe that their "inner child" (or unresolved parental relationships or repressed instincts, etc.) speak to them through dreams and intuitions—they too experience it and record it in writing. Modernity—despite having often, because of its particular moral belief system, characterized "mere beliefs" as subjective and emotion based and thus needing to be overridden by reason and knowledge—has in fact done little to change our human condition as fundamentally believing animals.

That moderns are every bit the believers our premodern ancestors were is also evident in the diversity of unverifiable assumptions and beliefs that govern so many of our modern life concerns. Many contemporary Americans, for example, believe that the object inside the uterus of a women between the time a man's sperm penetrates her egg and the time she gives birth (note the difficulty of even discussing this matter in terms that are not themselves deeply belief committed) is a living human person, an

---

10. George Thomas, *Revivalism and Cultural Change* (Chicago: University of Chicago Press, 1989).

unborn child, intimately linking the bodies and lives of generations and deserving without exception of all the love and protection that the most vulnerable members of our families and communities merit. Other contemporary Americans believe that this very same thing is a mass of tissue somewhat alien to the woman's own body that potentially deeply threatens her autonomy and well-being, which gives her every legitimate right to dispose of it. No amount of empirical evidence has been able to adjudicate between these views, and none likely will.[11] For in the end these views are essentially faith commitments to deep beliefs that turn out to be "true" only within larger frameworks of belief and practice built up themselves on deeper sets of unverifiable assumptions and beliefs. The only evidence that can "verify" either view proves to have already been constituted and framed by the deeper belief commitments from which the view itself is derived—which largely helps to explain the interminability of America's abortion debate. And the more "pragmatic" view that most Americans in the compromising middle end up adopting—that abortion really does end a human life and so is morally objectionable but that nobody except the mother has the right to make that final decision—itself could only possibly make sense in the context of certain baseline assumptions, beliefs, and practices that themselves cannot finally be verified or legitimated except by first committing to them. In this and very many other ways, we moderns stake our lives, our convictions, our politics, our associations on governing beliefs that no available independent or objective reason can

---

11. Although many attempts have been tried. Pro-life advocates, for example, advance evidence that fetuses not only look and behave remarkably like born human persons (for example, using fully formed fingers to suck thumbs), but also experience pain and struggle mightily against abortionists' attempts to terminate their lives. For their part, pro-choice activists point out that an entity that simply cannot survive on its own, apart from another person's biological support, can hardly be considered fully a person with a self possessing all of the rights pertaining to human personhood. Neither body of evidence, however, has managed to settle the debate, in part because the evidence itself is meaningless apart from other normative belief commitments and practices (concerning, for example, human autonomy and agency) that are required to make the evidence meaningful. And it is these conflicting normative beliefs that generate the differences over abortion in the first place.

conclusively verify. In the end, we simply believe them—as assumptions and commitments embedded in larger systems of belief and practice that make each of the particular beliefs seem perfectly valid.

The third characteristic about all of our suppositional assumptions and beliefs worth noting is that no "deeper," more objective or independent body of facts or knowledge exists to adjudicate between alternative basic assumptions and beliefs. For those of this sort are presuppositional starting points in which we (mostly unconsciously) place our trust and are not derived from other justifying grounds. To some degree, different assumptions and beliefs may be thought of as bearing up better or worse under the weight of the known or experienced facts. But the problem is that both what are taken to be "the facts" and our experiences are themselves significantly determined and made salient by the elemental assumptions and beliefs that function presuppositionally to constitute them. The ability of data to prove or disprove a theory, in other words, is problematic when the data themselves are always and profoundly theory-laden. It is our assumptions and beliefs that tell us what is relevant data and not, under what conditions, and why. For this reason, the empirically evident fact that the sun rises in the East in the morning and crosses the sky to set in the West itself could not decide whether the astronomical theory of Ptolemy or of Copernicus was correct—each theory was able, given its own presuppositions, to construe the evidence as consistent with its larger claims.[12] Thus normally the best anyone can do, at least in the short and medium run, is to own up to one's starting-point suppositions, to recognize them as such, and to work out with integrity their implications. Whether or not this must lead us to a relativist, skeptical, or nihilist position that despairs of ever adjudicating between alternative beliefs and worldviews is a question I take up at the end of the next chapter.

We see, then, that what any people, including ourselves, know about life and the world, about how life ought to be lived, is not founded on an indubitable, universal foundation of knowledge. These are not built on solid piles that have been driven down into a very bedrock of known reality that lies accessible beneath every human person. Rather all of our

---

12. Thomas Kuhn, *The Structure of Scientific Revolutions* (Chicago: University of Chicago Press, 1962). Also see Paul Feyerabend, *Against Method* (London: Verso, 1975).

knowledge and life practices—however obvious and well-founded they may seem to us—are built like large rafts on beams of particular trusted assumptions and beliefs that themselves float freely in the shifting seas of culture and history. And all of us, in our particular, historical communities of believers float together on those rafts, typically unable to see beyond our rafts to the open sea on which we float and thus accustomed to assuming our raft to be all that exists and is true.

Well-educated moderns are, of course, socialized to see other rafts. We are educated to recognize, tolerate, and appreciate a diversity of perspectives, paradigms, and cultures. At least to a point. For this modern, multivisioned self is itself, of course, an historically situated position constituted by faith commitments to particular basic assumptions and beliefs—about individuality, autonomy, cosmopolitanism, equality, relativity, self-expression, truth, and so on. And when occasions arise that threaten these trusted assumptions and beliefs, sophisticated, flexible, tolerant, liberal, well-educated moderns quickly show themselves to be the particularistically true believers they are—people committed, for the sake of establishing their very reality, to certain starting point suppositions as nonnegotiable.

Try, for example, persuading your cocktail party guests with all sincerity and persistence that human freedom is evil, that human rights do not exist, that some groups of people are inherently inferior to others, that one view of truth is absolutely correct and all others are false, that people need to learn to suppress and deny their own inner feelings and ideas, or that we would do better not to learn about the world beyond our own local people and boarders. Most likely, you will find it impossible to convince your guests that you are serious, since such ideas are so far removed from the realm of serious conceivable possibilities. But if you somehow *are* able to persuade them that you are serious, you will find that your arguments deeply violate your guests' very sacred belief commitments. How well they will be able to control their shock, indignation, and wrath will depend mostly on how many drinks they have consumed. Yet, in fact, neither they nor we can definitively and independently verify that these beliefs are actually right or wrong. They are rather right and wrong within particular knowledge systems that are built on trusted assumptions and presupposed beliefs that then make them "obviously" right or wrong.

Thus, for example, getting a committed neo-Nazi to adopt the position that Jews are not inherently inferior to "Aryan races" will not be accomplished by arguing empirical evidence. For all such evidence is itself constituted, framed, and made significant by the basic belief commitments that define the very matter under dispute. Actual Jews will rather obviously seem inferior to this Nazi. Rather, the Nazi must somehow more deeply come to see that his presuppositional beliefs are defective and then replace those with an alternative set of assumptions and beliefs—which will then make his previous empirical evidence about Jewish inferiority that was once so compelling to him now seem stupid and shameful. This process of change involves something much closer to undergoing a religious conversion than having one's mind altered in a rational argument about "the facts."

I am suggesting, then, that all human persons, no matter how well educated, how scientific, how knowledgeable, are, at bottom, *believers*. We are all necessarily trusting, believing animals, creatures who must and do place our faith in beliefs that *cannot themselves be verified except by means established by the presumed beliefs themselves*. The Muslim knows that Allah exists and commands because the Koran (a scripture revealed by Allah) tells her so. The agnostic knows that he cannot know whether God exists because his ideas about what we can possibly know (which are derived from nontheistic assumptions) tell him so. The empiricist knows that her research experiments and examinations provide truthful and reliable information about reality because she believes (based on empirically unverifiable empiricist assumptions) that sensory observations of the perceptible world provide reliable and accurate accounts of reality. The Buddhist (through Buddhist teachings) knows that our apprehension of ourselves as separate individuals is a delusion that must be annihilated in order to grasp the supreme Oneness of all of life and reach the bliss of nirvana.

To say that we are all finally believing animals is, in part, to say that we simply cannot function at all in our human lives without first committing ourselves to sets of assumptions and presupposed beliefs that make any functioning human life possible. We cannot do this any more than we can write a letter without an alphabet, vocabulary, and shared rules of grammar. If we perchance could imagine a human animal that is without any starting-point assumption or belief of the kind I have discussed—and what I have already said suggests that we cannot possibly imagine this, any more than we can imagine, say, dry water—then the animal we would have would be one that is incapacitated, paralyzed, without agency, lacking orientation, bereft of any bearings by which to proceed in life. Such a radically "unbelieving" human animal would have no place to begin, no categories, no reason to act, no identity. Only by believing in, committing to, placing faith in certain suppositions and propositions can we human animals ever be able to perceive, think, know, feel, will, choose, and act. Augustine of Hippo was more than a little right, then, in observing in the fourth century A.D.: "I believe that I may understand."[13]

To be clear, it is not that groups of humans cannot share a common reason. Nor that we cannot understand that a comprehendible reality beyond our consciousness really exists. Nor that we cannot come to discover extensively how aspects of that world works. It is simply that all of this knowledge and understanding, such as it is, does not rest on an epistemological foundation that is indubitable and universal and that can provide certain knowledge binding on everyone. All of our knowledge, rather, is situated within particularistic knowledge systems that are ultimately based on beliefs and assumptions that are nonuniversal and incapable of being independently and objectively verified.

From Philosophy to Sociology

Understanding ourselves as believing animals has implications for sociological work. First, it helps account for the tremendous diversity of human cultures and practices. Since knowledge is not founded on one universal and indubitable foundation but is rather built up from sets of starting-point assumptions and beliefs that are often very different from each other, humans are in a situation of tremendous world-defining openness that leads to a diversity of outcomes. Thus we find human belief communities for whom the natural world is sacred, possessed by spirits, and deserving the utmost reverence and other communities for whom nature

13. For two different discussions also related to this approach, see Wolterstorff, *Reason within the Bounds of Religion;* Hans-Georg Gadamer, *Truth and Method* (New York: Seabury Press, 1975).

is simply a lot of material resources waiting to be conquered and exploited for financial profit. We find communities for whom it is ultimately real that all people are and should be equal yet others for whom humanity is distributed in a hierarchy of differential importance and worth. Some believing communities see history as an endless cycle of recurring process finally going nowhere, while others are based on a belief in the real historical progress of civilization, morality, and humanity.

Recognizing that we humans are at bottom believing animals also helps to explain our persistent practice of sacralizing physical and mental objects. Humans are never simply believers in purely practical, functional terms. We are recurrently, almost impulsively believers in systems of knowledge and practice that involve sacreds and profanes. In and among the ordinary features of our lives, we set apart certain aspects as of such importance, power, or worth that they deserve our honor, our devotion, our protection. These we treat as sacrosanct, as inviolable, as holy— though not necessarily in strictly religious terms. In some communities, the sacred may be the spirits of ancestors or the cross of Christ. In other communities, what is sacred is the honor of noble warriors or the autonomy of the individual, the rights of private property, and the equality of all people.

However precisely we conceive and experience it, the sacred in any case involves in us strong emotional responses. We are highly sensitive about what is sacred to us, fervent, impassioned, and defensive if necessary. We are prepared to sacrifice for the sacred, in some cases to die and perhaps to kill for it. Again, not every sacred is religious.[14] The sacred may center on fatherland, liberty, science, the party, the proletariat, the environment, equality, the nation, sexual fulfillment. But inevitably there appear in human communities objects of belief of such worth and significance that they evoke the devotion, veneration, sacrifice, and assiduous protection of and from their believers.

Here lies a key link to this essay's observation that humans are fundamentally moral animals. We are moral animals, in part, because we are believing animals, and the character of our believing inevitably inclines toward sacralization, the differentiation of sacred from profane. Humans

14. For one secular account of the sacred, see, for instance, Ronald Dworkin, *Life's Domain* (New York: Vintage Books, 1994).

do not believe primarily in detached, abstract, practical modes. *Our be-livings are what create the conditions and shape of our very perceptions, identity, agency, orientation, purpose—in short, our selves, our lives, and our worlds as we know them.* They are therefore crucial to us, of fundamental importance. And these most basic belief commitments, the objects of our elemental faith and trust, frame for us our worldviews, cultures, ideologies, and religions—as variable as they may be, and as conscious or unconscious about them as we may be. From these basic life and world definitions and maps our moral orientations derive—our sense of good and bad, right and wrong, worthy and unworthy, just and unjust, noble and shameful. And as these moral discriminations are rooted in the kind of presuppositional, life-constituting beliefs and assumptions discussed earlier, we do not and cannot relate to them finally as simply the products or reflections of our own opinions, preferences, inclinations, or desires. They come to stand in relation to us, rather, as above and beyond, objectively independent standards positioned to render judgment on our opinions, preferences, and desires.

Thus when the patriotic and loyal soldier sacrifices his life in battle for his comrades or country, he is not simply the victim of unfortunate circumstances. More profoundly, he is enacting the calling and obligations of an integrated moral order of nation, honor, and comradeship. To have done otherwise (even if nobody else would have ever known that he chose survival over sacrifice) would not simply mean being troubled in future years with occasional pangs of regret or guilt—hardly enough to motivate someone to die for others. It would, for this kind of soldier, more importantly mean evading one of life's most sacred callings, miscarrying one's duty in a crucial moment of definition and testing, dishonoring country in cowardice and selfishness, and failing to love and honor one's comrades-in-arms. In short, it would be a profound moral failing. Likewise, the contemporary insurance salesman who decides in midlife to divorce his wife, move to the Rockies, take up hang-gliding and dog-sledding, and party with young women is not simply choosing appropriate means to achieving his personal preferences. More fundamentally, he is enacting a set of deep, largely unconscious normative beliefs about individual autonomy, masculine self-expression, and human self-fulfillment—elemental assumptions ultimately about the nature of human personhood and the character of human flourishing. And given his full (even if largely unconscious) embrace of these beliefs, for this man to have instead stayed home, endured his unsatisfying wife, repressed his desires for outdoor adventures and sexual escapades, and continued simply to try to win his company's quarterly sales awards would have not only been frustrating and disappointing but would have also been cowardly, a denial of his true self, a transgression of the way things ought to be. Which is to say, it would have been a violation of a moral order.

The final sociological implication of the recognition that we humans are believers at our core is that we will never really understand human social life if we do not pay close attention to the content and function of the beliefs that humans together hold and build their lives on. Certain accounts of the human animal that do not accord importance to their ultimate condition as believers, but instead posit some universal, primordial drive or motivation, claim that we can afford to disregard human beliefs and their cultural derivatives. These accounts, which typically descend from the naturalistic, often utilitarian tradition of Western social theory, have many expressions: behaviorism, neoclassical economics, rational choice theory, exchange theory, artificial intelligence theory, public choice theory, sociobiology, and so on. At their core is the belief that human consciousness and action can be properly understood with reference to one foundational, universal, inalienable drive or interest—the pursuit of pleasure, the maximizing of rewards and minimizing of costs, the quest for social dominance, genetic reproduction, et cetera. What all of these theories badly miss, however, is the variable, world-open, creative, trusting, and believing condition at the core of human animals that generates a variety of socially constructed realities in diverse human communities, which constitute, mediate, and govern human consciousness, action, and institutions. In short, what they badly miss is the necessity for any good sociology to be a deeply and thoroughly *cultural* sociology— despite all the messiness and indeterminacy that entails.

Implicit in the account of human animals offered here, in other words, is the recognition that the starting-point presuppositions, assumptions, beliefs, and commitments of human communities actually have enormous ramifications for the character of those communities' practices, perceptions, and institutions. In simple terms, basic beliefs have consequences. It matters a great deal in understanding social structures of inequality over the long run, for example, whether human communities suppose fundamentally that people through reincarnation are rewarded and punished for how they live their lives over many lives; that a common humanity of rationality, morality, and dignity has been created "in the image of God"; or that because there is no God all things are in fact (a)morally permissible. It matters in the formation of political life whether believing communities presume that history is an endless, unalterable cycle of repetition and futility or that history is the progressive story of valiant activists winning the ever-growing expansion of freedom, equality, and brotherhood. For that matter, it matters enormously for political life simply whether human communities can conceive and believe the categorical entities "vassal," "subject," "folk," "rabble," "compatriot," "citizens," or "constituent." For one can have a certain political (or economic or familial or religious) social structure only after the constituent cultural elements of that structure are first imagined and believed.[15]

Therefore, sociological research programs that are fundamentally naturalistic, utilitarian, antimentalist, or noncultural will inevitably fail to understand human persons, consciousness, actions, and institutions. They are projects very badly gauged to address their subject of study and so necessarily have ended and will end in frustration, if not dead-ended failure. Properly understood, they are actually themselves historically situated moral projects, built up from presuppositions and assumptions that cannot be independently verified, and championed by devotees who (more

---

15 Thus William Sewell Jr.'s *Work and Revolution in France* (New York: Cambridge University Press, 1980) has shown that the French Revolution is explicable, not simply because "structural" factors, such as state fiscal debt patterns, caused it—as Theda Skocpol's *States and Social Revolutions* (New York: Cambridge University Press, 1979) would have it—but instead, crucially, because cultural categories that make revolution conceivable and sensible were constructed and embraced by relevant actors. See William H. Sewell Jr., "Ideologies and Social Revolutions: Reflections on the French Case," *Journal of Modern History* 57, no. 1 (1985): 57–85; Theda Skocpol, "Cultural Idioms and Political Ideologies in the Revolutionary Reconstruction of State Power: A Rejoinder to Sewell," *Journal of Modern History* 57, no. 1 (1985): 86–96. Also see Craig Calhoun, "Introduction: Social Issues in the Study of Culture," *Comparative Social Research* 11 (1989): 15–16. Relevant here as well is Benedict Anderson's *Imagined Communities: Reflections on the Origin and Spread of Nationalism* (London: Verso, 1983); and Robert Wuthnow, *Communities of Discourse* (Cambridge: Harvard University Press, 1989).

or less consciously) believe in the moral worth of the projects. This—much more than objective verifiability, intellectual plausibility, or empirical predictive payoff—is what finally explains the appeal and persistence of these moral/scientific projects. They embody and reinforce key elements of the secular Enlightenment story—the autonomously choosing individual, a godless universe composed only of energy and matter, a comprehensive and universal science of Man, the economic "laws" of the free marketplace, and so on. At bottom it is widespread belief in a particular moral order and the project it implies that so forcefully propels these theoretical visions.

Modern Parochialism

If the idea that all human persons are at bottom believing animals is to us novel or incredible, it is most likely so not because this does not well describe human persons. Rather, it is most likely because the deep assumptions and beliefs of the particular, historical system of knowledge and practice that encompasses and patterns most aspects of our lives—modern liberal democratic capitalism—have become our only horizon. This is the raft beyond which we cannot see. Modern liberal democratic capitalism, and the cultural ontology that floats it, is now, through the process of globalization and marketing, colonizing most regions of the world and most aspects of our lives.

We are very familiar with the story of how a hegemonic medieval Catholic feudalism unified the worldview of the "Middle Ages," making it nearly impossible for peasants and lords alike to imagine anything other. That world became for its inhabitants fixed, unified, total.

What may be less clear to us today is that liberal democratic capitalism is effecting a similar outcome. Its suppositional beliefs, its deeply trusted assumptions, its elemental cultural ontology have become nearly invisible to us precisely because it has become ubiquitous and dominant. We thus mistake its set of historically recent, culturally relative, and reasonably contestable assumptions about the nature and purpose of human persons and society for the way things actually are. Ironically, the implausible nature of the believing animals thesis to us is itself the most powerful substantiation of the very thesis itself. For most of us are such committed and trusting believers in the basic assumptions that constitute our liberal democratic capitalist world that we cannot even recognize our own believing as such. The world we bring into being through believing has for us become fixed, unified, total. We are thus not in the end very different in this condition than the medieval peasant from whom the Enlightenment promised to raise and deliver us. We are finally the very same kind of animal, lacking solid foundations, and so building up our lives as firmly as we can on trust and faith.

FOUR

LIVING NARRATIVES

Many years ago, our human ancestors huddled around fires listening to shamans and elders telling imaginative stories by which they made sense of their world and their lives in it. They told myths about the world's origins, and about how they as peoples came to be. They told legends about mighty heroes of old, about overcoming great adversity, about visions of the future. They narrated tales of moral struggle, about people good and bad, and about what happens to naughty children. They recounted myths about fairies, spirits, gods, and powerful cosmic forces. By narrating such fictional stories, our ancestors recounted meaningful explanations of a world that was to them mysterious and dangerous—and entertained themselves in the process. As primitives, telling such stories, myths, and legends was the only way they knew how to explain the world and contemplate how to live in it. And such was the condition of traditional human societies of all kinds up until a few hundred years ago.

But all of that has changed. We moderns no longer have to huddle around fires telling fanciful myths about creations, floods, trials, conquests, and hoped-for paradises. Science, industry, rationality, and technology have dispelled the darkness and ignorance that once held the human race captive to its fanciful fables. Today, through progress, enlightenment, and cultural evolution, we now possess positive knowledge, scientific facts, rational analyses. We no longer need to be a people of ballads and legends, for we are a people of periodic tables, technical manuals, genetic maps, and computer codes. We may tell fables to our children about wolves and witches and arks. But the adult world is one of modern, scientific information, facts, and knowledge. We have left behind myths and legends. We are now educated, rational, analytical. Indeed, by struggling to break out of the fear and ignorance of our ancestral myth-making past into the clear daylight of rational, scientific knowledge, we have opened up for the human race a future of greater prosperity, longevity, and happiness.

Such is the story we moderns—huddled around our televisions and computer work stations—like to tell each other. This is the dominant narrative by which we make sense of our world and the purpose of our lives in it.

The point here is not that modernity's story is false. Narratives, myths, and fables can be true, in their way. The point, rather, is that for all of our science, rationality, and technology, we moderns are no less the makers, tellers, and believers of narrative construals of existence, history, and purpose than were our forebears at any other time in human history. But more than that, we not only continue to be animals who make stories but also animals who are *made by* our stories. We tell and retell narratives that themselves come fundamentally to constitute and direct our lives. We, every bit as much as the most primitive or traditional of our ancestors, are animals who most fundamentally understand what reality is, who we are, and how we ought to live by locating ourselves within the larger narratives and metanarratives that we hear and tell, and that constitute what is for us real and significant.[1]

---

1. See Paul Ricoeur, *Time and Narrative, Volume 1*, trans. by Kathleen McLaughlin and David Pellauer (Chicago: University of Chicago Press, 1984); *Time and Narrative, Volume 2*, trans. by Kathleen McLaughlin and David Pellauer (Chicago: University of Chicago Press, 1985); *Time and Narrative, Volume 3*, trans. by Kathleen Blamey and David Pellauer (Chicago: University of Chicago Press, 1988); Alasdair MacIntyre, *After Virtue* (Notre Dame, Ind.: University of Notre Dame Press, 1981), 204–25; Douglas Ezzy, "Theorizing Narrative Identity," *Sociological Quarterly* 39, no. 2 (1998): 239–52; Anthony Paul Kerby, *Narrative and the Self* (Bloomington: Indiana University Press, 1991); Jerome Bruner, "Life as Narrative," *Social Research* 54, no. 1 (1987): 11–32. Miller Mair, "Psychology as Storytelling,"

What then exactly is narrative? Narrative is a form of communication that arranges human actions and events into organized wholes in a way that bestows meaning on the actions and events by specifying their inter-active or cause-and-effect relations to the whole. Narratives are much more than chronicles, which merely list discrete events by placing them on timelines. Narratives seek to convey the significance and meaning of events by situating their interaction with or influence on other events and actions in a single, interrelated account. Narratives, thus, always have a point, are always about the explanation and meaning of events and actions in human life, however simple these may be.[2]

All narratives include a handful of essential elements. First, narratives have a set of characters or actors who are the subjects and objects of action. Second, narratives involve plots with typically structured sequences of beginning, middle, and end—although the plot may not necessarily present its story in sequential order. The plot's beginning generally sets

---

International Journal of Personal Construct Psychology 1 (1988): 125–37. Also see Hans-Georg Gadamer, *Truth and Method* (New York: Seabury Press, 1975).

2. Here and in the following paragraph I am following Donald Polkinghorne, *Narrative Knowing and the Human Sciences* (Albany: State University of New York Press, 1988); George Steinmetz, "Reflections on the Role of Social Narratives in Working-Class Formation: Narrative Theory in the Social Sciences," *Social Science History* 16, no. 4 (Winter 1992); Margaret Somers, "Narrativity, Narrative Identity, and Social Action," *Social Science History* 16, no. 4 (Winter 1992); Lewis Hinchman and Sandra Hinchman, introduction to *Memory, Identity, Community: The Idea of Narrative in the Human Sciences* (Albany: State University of New York Press, 1997); David Maines, "Narrative's Moment and Sociology's Phenomena: Toward a Narrative Sociology," *Sociological Quarterly* 34, no. 1 (1993): 17–38. Also see Theodore Sarbin (ed.), *Narrative Psychology: The Storied Nature of Human Conduct* (New York: Praeger, 1986); Joseph de Rivera and Theodore Sarbin (eds.), *Believed-In Imaginings: The Narrative Construction of Reality* (Washington, D.C.: American Psychological Association, 1998); Kenneth Gergen and Mary Gergen, "Narratives of the Self," in Hinchman and Hinchman, *Memory, Identity, Community;* David Yamane, "Narrative and Religious Experience," *Sociology of Religion* 61 (2000): 171–89; Molly Patterson and Kristen Renwick Monroe, "Narratives in Political Science," *Annual Review of Political Science* (Palo Alto, Calif.: Annual Reviews, 1998); Terri Orbuch, "People's Accounts Count: The Sociology of Accounts," *Annual Review of Sociology* (Palo Alto, Calif.: Annual Reviews, 1997).

the story's context and subject, the middle introduces a significant problem or conflict that the characters must address, and the end involves some outcome or resolution of the problem or conflict. Third, narratives convey significant points. They are designed to draw the audience to an explanation, a revelation, and understanding, or an insight about life and the world. For this reason, with even the most elementary of narratives, audiences will press storytellers to complete unfinished narratives, to get to their stories' *point*. So, if we meet in the hall and I tell you, "I drove downtown today to pick up Billy's prescription, and was looking for a parking space" and then stop, you will probably reply, "Yeah? So?" You thus oblige me to complete my narrative—"Well, it took a long time because it was so crowded. But then the nicest man who was waiting in his car outside the store saw that I was having trouble and offered to let me have his space. I was so touched"—and so get to its point: even in a difficult world there are good people who can brighten one's day and make life so much more enjoyable.

In order to construct a narrative, the storyteller selects specific events from the past that serve as the vehicles of commentary and meaning-making. Not all possible past happenings are important to recount, only those that render a particular story by emplotting selected elements in a way that conveys the larger intended moral and meaning. For in a narrative world not all "facts" matter. What matters is the more significant story running through, over, and under "the facts," the story that itself constitutes what is a fact, what it is that matters.

But wait just a minute. What is this talk of narratives? The "postmodern" condition, we have been instructed of late, has brought with it the suspicion of, perhaps even *the end* of, coherent narratives, especially "grand narratives." Postmodern people are the kind who simply cannot believe in the metanarratives offered by, say, Marxism, Christianity, and liberalism. The expansiveness, coherence, and claims to universality of these grand stories have become simply incredible to those who have lived through and beyond modernity.[3]

However fashionable this notion has become in some intellectual cir-

---

3. Jean-Francois Lyotard, *The Postmodern Condition: A Report on Knowledge*, trans. Geoff Bennington and Brian Massumi (Minneapolis: University of Minnesota Press, 1984).

cles, the suggestion of this chapter is that it simply is not true. The human animal is a moral, believing animal—inescapably so. And the larger cultural frameworks within which the morally oriented believings of the human animal make sense are most deeply narrative in form. Of course, postmodernism itself is a narrative, hardly providing an escape from story-based knowledge and meaning. But the problem in its claims about the end of metanarratives run still deeper than this self-contradiction. Postmodernism simply underestimates the vitality and appeal of certain narratives—particularly in America, of the modern story of progress and liberal freedom; and, for many, of the Christian story. Those metanarratives and their associated narratives are very much alive and well—however coherent or less than perfectly coherent they are. Progress and liberal freedom, in particular, are still the driving spirit, vision, and energy of contemporary public culture and social institutions. Postmodern claims on this point, therefore, cannot be taken seriously. We have no more dispensed with grand narratives than with the need for lungs to breath with. We cannot live without stories, big stories finally, to tell us what is real and significant, to know who we are, where we are, what we are doing, and why.

Narratives to Live By

With this in mind, we can begin to see how narratives are composed and how they work, by examining first a very familiar and often very meaningful story to most United States citizens, what we might call the *American Experiment narrative*:

> Once upon a time, our ancestors lived in an Old World where they were persecuted for religious beliefs and oppressed by established aristocracies. Land was scarce, freedoms denied, and futures bleak. But then brave and visionary men like Columbus opened up a New World, and our freedom-loving forefathers crossed the ocean to carve out of a wilderness a new civilization. Through bravery, ingenuity, determination, and goodwill, our forebears forged a way of life where men govern themselves, believers worship in freedom, and where anyone can grow rich and become president. This America is genuinely new, a clean break from the past, a historic experiment in freedom and democracy standing as a city on a hill shining

a beacon of hope to guide a dark world into a future of prosperity and liberty. It deserves our honor, our devotion, and possibly the commitment of our very lives for its defense.

Such is the story many readers of this book have been told from earliest days by parents, teachers, textbooks, civic leaders, and politicians alike. It is a story that provides untold millions a most significant collective identity, sense of place in the world, orientation to the good in life, basis of solidarity with strangers, ordering of time and emotions through national holidays and their ritual celebrations, and more. Without this narrative rendering of reality to tell and retell, very many Americans would confront the world with profound confusion and disorientation. For one thing, it would mean little to think of themselves as "Americans." But with this national narrative constituting our individual and collective identities and practices, we together begin to know who we are, why we exist, how we should spend our lives, and what duty calls us to when we and our way of life are threatened or attacked.

By comparison, we might examine a very different narrative, perhaps equally powerful in the world today, that I will call the *Militant Islamic Resurgence narrative*—the story told by radical Muslims who are determined (by violence if necessary) to reorder the existing geopolitical world:

> Once upon a time, even while Europe was stumbling through its medieval darkness, a glorious Muslim empire and civilization led the world in all manner of science, art, technology, and culture. Islam prospered for many centuries under faithful submission to Allah. But then, crusading Infidels from the Northwest invaded the land of Islam and over five hundred years have progressively conquered, divided, and subjugated us. Once glorious, Islam has now suffered endless humiliations, infidelities, and corruptions through Western colonialism, secularism, socialism, communism, mass consumerism, feminism, and eroticism. Now arrogant Western infidelity desecrates the sacred lands of Mohamed and Palestine with its armies, and by backing our Jewish enemies. But today the tide is finally turning. Islam has awoken and is now returning to fidelity and glory, with a new vision of devotion to faith. All believers must submit themselves to Allah and devote their lives to a holy war to drive out infidels both at home and abroad.

This story makes complete sense to tens of millions of Muslims throughout the world, although, with few exceptions, it is implausible for most Americans. Indeed, this narrative is a "counternarrative" that inverts the

American Experiment story, renarrating history so that America is a source of evil and not good in the world.[4] Thus the U.S. responses to the attacks of September 11, 2001, were not simply about homeland security, concern for stability in the Middle East, and so on. Most profoundly, the U.S. response from the first day was a campaign to vindicate America's national narrative.

Narratives, however, need not only be the stories of nations and political movements. Larger, more encompassing metanarratives can plot *all* of reality and its meaning in stories. The *Christian metanarrative* is one familiar case; it runs something like this:

> A personal, loving, holy God created the heavens and earth for his own glory, making humans in his very image, and establishing a relationship of care and friendship with humanity. Tragically, however, humans in pride have chosen to rebel against and reject God, the source of all life and happiness, thus plunging the world into all manner of evil, death, and spiritual blindness. But the love and grace of God is more powerful and determined than the sin of humanity, so through Israel God continued his covenant relationship to redeem the world from its sin. Rather than allowing creation to reap death and utter destruction as the full and just consequence of sin, God himself became human and freely took upon himself those evil consequences. Through the undeserved crucifixion and resurrection of Jesus Christ, God conquered death, set aright the broken relationship, and opened a way for the redemption of creation. God now calls all people to respond through his Spirit to this divine love and grace by repenting from sin and walking in a new life of friendship with and obedience to God in the church and in the world. Those who persist in their denial of God's love will finally get exactly what they want, the end of which is death. But those who embrace God will enjoy and worship him together as his people forever in a new heaven and earth.

This Christian metanarrative, like those of most religions, tells an all-encompassing story about the origin and purpose of the cosmos, about the nature and destiny of humanity, about fundamental moral order. It offers a master narrative, a metanarrative that seeks to govern all other narratives below and within it.

4. See Steinmetz, "Reflections on the Role of Social Narratives in Working-Class Formation," 496.

Human cultures abound with narratives and metanarratives of varying scope and significance. The following are some very brief recountings of a few other major narratives familiar in Western culture:

The Capitalist Prosperity narrative. For most of human history, the world's material production was mired in oppressive and inefficient economic systems such as primitive communalism, slavery, feudalism, mercantilism, and, more recently, socialism and communism. In eighteenth-century Europe and America, however, enterprising men hit upon the keys to real prosperity: private property rights, limited government, the profit motive, capital investment, the free market, rational contracts, technological innovation—in short, economic freedom. The capitalist revolution has produced more wealth, social mobility, and well-being than any other system could possibly imagine or deliver. Nevertheless, capitalism is continually beset by utopian egalitarians, government regulators, and antientrepreneurial freeloaders who foolishly seek to fetter its dynamic power with heavy-handed state controls. All who care for a world of freedom and prosperity will remain vigilant in defense of property rights, limited government, and the free market.

The Progressive Socialism narrative. In the most primitive days, before the rise of private property, humans lived in communities of material sharing and equality. But for most of subsequent human history, with the rise of private property, the world's material production has been mired in oppressive and exploitative economic systems, such as slavery, feudalism, mercantilism, and capitalism. The more history has progressed, the more ownership of the means of production have become centralized, and the more humanity has suffered deprivation and injustice. As the calamitous contradictions of capitalism began to intensify in the nineteenth century, however, a revolutionary vanguard emerged who envisioned a society of fraternity, justice, and equality. They proclaimed the abolition of private property, the socialization of production, and the distribution of goods not according to buying power but according to need. Right-wing tycoons and magnates who have everything to lose to the cause of justice fight against the socialist movement with all their power and wealth. But the power of workers in solidarity for justice will eventually achieve the utopia of prosperity and equality. Workers of the world, unite! You have nothing to lose but your chains!

The Expressive Romantic narrative. Once upon a time, people were free to experience the exhilarating power of nature, to assert their primitive selves, to shout raucously, to dance wildly, to fight hard, to love harder. They were noble, authentic, primal, unrestrained. The encroachments of civilization, however, have gradually domesticated humanity, smothering our authentic, primeval selves under blankets of repressive and artificial manners, refinements, restraints, proprieties, denials, and formal rationalities. Modern people hardly know any more who they are, what they feel, how to express their will and passions. Only a few free thinkers have broken through the suffocating restraint, and at great cost, but they point the way to authentic life and self-expression. They flaunt convention. They walk the less trod roads. They get in touch with their deepest selves. They beat drums. They splatter paint and scrawl poetry. They run naked through forests. They dance in the rain. They party wildly, altering states of consciousness. They are not bound by the bourgeois mores and manners that extinguish the human spirit. They fear not the Dionysian orgy, nor violent rebellion, nor bohemian isolation. They are troubled souls on wild and lonely quests, yet are society's only hope for authentic and expressive living, perhaps even for redemption itself through pain and art.

The Scientific Enlightenment narrative. For most of human history, people have lived in the darkness of ignorance and tradition, driven by fear, believing in superstitions. Priests and lords preyed on such ignorance, and life was wearisome and short. Ever so gradually, however, and often at great cost, inventive men have endeavored better to understand the natural world around them. Centuries of such inquiry eventually led to a marvelous Scientific Revolution that radically transformed our methods of understanding nature. What we know now as a result is based on objective observation, empirical fact, and rational analysis. With each passing decade, science reveals increasingly more about the earth, our bodies, our minds. We have come to possess the power to transform nature and ourselves. We can fortify health, relieve suffering, and prolong life. Science is close to understanding the secret of life and maybe eternal life itself. Of course, forces of ignorance, fear, irrationality, and blind faith still threaten the progress of science. But they must be resisted at all costs. For unfettered science is our only hope for true enlightenment and happiness.

Much of the social discourse of the West for the last two hundred years and even today finds it roots in the struggles between these major rival narratives.

Note that there are many ways to recount these grand narratives. The foregoing versions are only one possible rendition of each. Still, most versions will follow similar basic story lines. Furthermore, any given individual who is in fact under the influence of a narrative may not fully recognize all elements of its story in his or her own life. A modern youth acting out the Expressive Romantic narrative, for example, may not actually be considering beating drums or splattering paint or running naked through forests. That does not matter. That does not reduce the power of the narrative in and over their life. It is not necessary for individuals to be fully aware of or articulate about the details or variants of the historical narratives that shape their lives or to represent in their particular experience every element of the narrative story line. Most people relate to their narratives not as literary critics or analytical philosophers but as believing actors swept up in the movement of grand historical drama. Their lives are embedded within and expressive of big stories, whether or not they can recognize every detail of any version of the story in their present life.

Note too that these narratives I have told here in general terms. People often retell them with more concrete actors in action. The Scientific Enlightenment narrative, for example, is told with its actors not being simply "inventive men" but Ben Franklin, Thomas Edison, Albert Einstein, Bill Gates. The Progressive Socialism narrative may be told in terms of Eugene Debs, Fidel, perhaps even Uncle Harry's injury on the job that prompted a successful strike.

As an aside, what is striking about these major Western narrative traditions is how closely their plots parallel and sometimes mimic the Christian narrative. Hardly below their surfaces are the common threads of a secularized theology—a fall or awakening into sin, the redemptive quest, conversion and transformation, temptations to backslide, persevering in salvation, and an expectant hope for a final happiness and fulfillment. So deep did Christianity's wagon wheels wear into the ground of Western culture and consciousness, that nearly every secular wagon that has followed—no matter how determined to travel a different road—has found it nearly impossible not to ride in the same tracks of the faith of old. Such is the power of moral order in deeply forming culture and story.

But I should not overemphasize the consistent patterns across narratives. For the West is only one civilization, and even within the West contrary stories have emerged. Outside of the West, many other narratives have shaped civilizations and cultures. So as not to belabor the point, I will recite only two. The first we may call the *Divine Life and Afterlife narrative*, different versions of which appear to have undergirded much of the politics, everyday life practices, and funeral rites in ancient Egypt.

> Once upon a time, the universe was created by the sun-god, Ra, who appeared out of primeval chaos and created the air god Shu and his wife Tefnut; to these were born the sky-goddess Nut and the earth-god Geb, who in turn bore Osiris, Isis, and Set. Osiris became king and judge of the dead, and god of the waters of the Nile, the grain harvest, the moon, and the sun—the beloved protector of all, both poor and rich. One day, however, Osiris was murdered by his brother, Set. But he was restored to life by his wife, Isis, and so became the great god of the eternal persistence of life. Osiris was also avenged by his son, Horus, revealing the triumph of good over evil. All creation is thus spiritual in origin. We humans are born mortal, but we contain within ourselves the seed of the divine, which, if we avoid evil, can reach its full potential in us after death. Our purpose in this life is to nourish that seed, and, if successful, we will be rewarded with eternal life in the next world and be reunited with our divine origin. If we worship the gods, live honorable lives, avoid evil, and follow proper procedures in death, our souls—our "ka" and "ba"—will live eternally in the Underworld.

A second significant non-Western narrative, which we may name the *Destined Unity with Brahman narrative,* associated with Hinduism, has profoundly shaped the dominant culture and society of the Indus valley for millennia:

> From the origin of eternal time, the one all-pervasive Supreme Being, the immense, unifying, immanent and transcendent force of Brahman, has created, preserved, and dissolved the universe in endless cycles. All of reality is moving toward an ultimate unity with the cosmic Absolute. However, bad karma, the moral and physical law of cause and effect, works to obstruct the path to salvation and the liberation. Each of us must therefore come to understand the truth and strive, through the way of works, knowledge, and devotion as spiritual paths to God-realization, to resolve, through cycles of reincarnation, our good and bad karmic results. Through rituals, self-reflection, and devotion to one's gods, one will work to reach one's final destiny of unity with Brahman, find morality, and reach nirvana, the peaceful escape from the cycle of reincarnation.

Many readers of this book may find it hard to imagine living lives naturally and meaningfully formed by these two narratives, or many others we might retell, but that is because in those cases they are other people's stories. Those other people whose lives are constituted by those other stories would no doubt have just as difficult a time imagining living meaningful lives out of the Christian or American Experiment or Expressive Romantic narratives that many of us are familiar with.

Different narratives and metanarratives, we might note, are more or less compatible with each other depending on their plots, actors, and other elements. Some narratives fit together only very uncomfortably, if at all—the American Experiment and Militant Islamic Resurgence being but one example. Others mesh together quite well. The American Experiment narrative, for instance, has always easily been integrated into the larger Christian metanarrative. With only a few shifts in imagery, the Old World is Egypt; the Atlantic is the Jordan River; America is a promised land; Americans are God's chosen people, a new Israel; George Washington is America's Moses; political and economic (and, for some, moral) liberty is salvation; U.S. foreign policy fulfills our evangelical mission, and so on. To be sure, there are no definite formulas or schemas predicting how narratives will relate to each other. Human culture and history are simply too loaded with openness, creativity, contingency, and messiness to identify a single deep structure beneath and between our narratives.[5] Some narratives derive from others. Other narratives oppose yet others. And some narratives both derive from and oppose others. Some narratives emplot quite different dimensions of life, others partially overlap, while yet others seem to compete with each other as framings of reality. There are no positive laws in narrative to be discovered, only historical, interpretive analysis to conduct.

Another point about narratives that is important to see is that narratives are transposable and therefore can be applied creatively to varieties

5. Here I part ways with Northrop Frye, *The Anatomy of Criticism* (Princeton, N.J.: Princeton University Press, 1957); and, in a different way, part with Talcott Parsons's "pattern variables" approach to culture, as in, for example, Talcott Parsons and Edward Shils, "Values, Motives, and Systems of Action," in Parsons and Shils (eds.), *Toward a General Theory of Action* (New York: Harper, 1951).

of historical situations, whether intentionally or not. The Exodus story about the liberation of the ancient Israelites from the oppressive hand of Egypt's pharaoh, for example, has served as a narrative template for innumerable movements of liberation and revolution over centuries in the West. It was the transposability of narratives that made the ancient Hebrew Exodus an entirely relevant story, for example, to mid-nineteenth-century American abolitionists and mid-twentieth-century civil rights activists. Likewise, it was the transposability of narratives that made the early New England Puritan jeremiads—sermons about original calling, subsequent unfaithfulness, and need for sincere repentance—the discursive framework of many important subsequent movements, from Sabbath laws campaigns to the protest movement against the Vietnam War. These and many other key narratives have exerted huge influences, through their transposable adaptability, on the defining cultural categories that have shaped action in the West and in America.[6]

Finally, the discussion thus far has emphasized big narratives about the world and the cosmos. But narratives operate at many levels and in many layers. People's lives are also always constituted and guided by smaller, sometimes autobiographical narratives of personal existence and experience. Narratives not only provide "big picture" frameworks of life but likewise help to construct more specific and personal accounts and themes of meaning, purpose, and explanation in life. Big narratives often have links of meaning to smaller narratives, but not always or clearly so. Thus people's lives and identities may not only be situated within the American Experiment or Christian narratives, for instance, but at other levels their experience is viewed and explained through narratives about the loss of jobs, political activism, immigration, the fairness of laws, encounters of love or violence, recovery from trauma, motherhood, organizational identities, sexual experiences, religious conversions, and more.[7] This multilevel

6. See, for example, Northrop Frye, *The Great Code* (Toronto: Academic Press, 1982).

7. See, for example, Douglas Ezzy, *Narrating Unemployment* (Aldershot: Ashgate, 2001); Christian Smith, *Resisting Reagan* (Chicago: University of Chicago Press, 1996), 203–8; Mary Chamberlain, *Narratives of Exile and Return* (New York: St. Martin's Press, 1997); Grant Reeher, *Narratives of Justice: Legislators' Beliefs*

and multilayered nature of narratives helps to account for the pervasiveness and centrality of narratives in the composition, direction, and interpretation of human life.

Narrative, Identity, and the Sacred

Emile Durkheim rightly taught that every social order has at its core the sacred. Social orders are not merely populations carrying on instrumentally functional institutions. Rather, social orders ultimately are held together and set into motion by particular ideas and ideals about themselves that comprise their collective identities. It is these collective identities that give social orders their essential locations, orientations, and significance in the larger world. "A society can neither create itself nor recreate itself," wrote Durkheim, "without at the same time creating an ideal. . . . For a society is not made up merely of the mass of individuals who compose it, the ground which they occupy, the things which they use, and the movements which they perform, but above all of the idea which it forms of itself."[8] And the center of any collective identity is not instrumental functionality but believed-in ideals and images that are sacred—that are, for the social order, set apart, hallowed, protected, inviolable.

Durkheim's reductionistic suggestion that all religions are ultimately nothing but the worship of sacred social ideals is highly debatable. The connection of the sacred and the social, however, when viewed through

---

about Distributive Fairness (Ann Arbor: University of Michigan Press, 1996); Ann Swidler, *Talk of Love* (Chicago: University of Chicago Press, 2001); Marita Sturken, *Narratives of Recovery* (Hanover, N.H.: University Press of New England, 1999); Gerald Cromer, *Narratives of Violence* (Burlington, Vt.: Ashgate, 2001); Brenda Daly and Maureen Reddy (eds.), *Narrating Mothers* (Knoxville: University of Tennessee Press, 1991); Barbara Czarniawska-Joerges, *Narrating the Organization: Dramas of Institutional Identity* (Chicago: University of Chicago Press, 1997); Sharon Thompson, *Going All the Way: Teenager Girls' Tales of Sex, Romance, and Pregnancy* (New York: Hill and Wang, 1995); Peter Stromberg, *Language and Self-Transformation: A Study of the Christian Conversion Narrative* (Cambridge: Cambridge University Press, 1993).

8. Emile Durkheim, *The Elementary Forms of Religious Life* (New York: Free Press, 1915), 470.

the other end of the telescope, may hit closer to the mark: that all social orders are in a sense ultimately religious, in having sacreds at heart, in the form of sacrosancts set apart from the ordinary and profane through and by which the social orders live, move, and have their being. This is arguably true in the historical sense that civilizations are repeatedly founded on religions. According to Peter Berger, "Originally all cosmization had a sacred character. This remains true through most of human history. . . . Viewed historically, most of man's worlds have been sacred worlds. Indeed, it appears likely that only by way of the sacred was it possible for man to conceive of a cosmos in the first place."[9] It is also true in a cultural sense, that the broader categories of interpretive meaning that animate any society are organized at bottom in relation to sacred moral order. This is precisely the point that Robert Bellah, for example, makes in his piece "Is There a Common American Culture?"—that America is religiously committed to the sacredness of the individual conscience, whether in the form of Roger Williams's sectarian Baptist faith or of the modern, secular, liberal, political activist.[10]

But we should note that the sacred ideals that define social orders do not float freely in the sky of ideas, like arbitrary clumps of ideas and beliefs that somehow happen to get invested with religious qualities. Rather, the sacred at the heart of any social order is always embedded in and arising from its collective narratives. It is the story that constructs the ideal. It is the narrative that defines the sacred. Thus the individual conscience is sacred in America not because of some random happen-

---

9. Peter Berger, *The Sacred Canopy* (New York: Doubleday, 1967), 27. Also see Christopher Dawson, *Progress and Religion* (Washington, D.C.: Catholic University of America Press, 2001); *Religion and the Rise of Western Culture* (New York: Sheed and Ward, 1950).

10. Robert Bellah, "Is There a Common American Culture?" *Journal for the American Academy of Religion* 66, no. 3 (1998): 613–25. There also seems to be a point of connection here to the neo-institutionalist argument that formal organizations do not so much act rationally as operate according to organizational myths of rationality that are adopted and dramatized ceremonially; see, for example, John Meyer and Brian Rowan, "Institutionalized Organizations: Formal Structure as Myth and Ceremony," *American Journal of Sociology* 83, no. 2 (1977): 340–63.

stance but because the larger American Experiment story narrates it for us as sacred. It is not some abstract and random national commitment per se that makes it so but rather the particular national recounting of what is true and important in the narrative form of actors, context, plot, action, conflict, and resolution.

This is in part what it means to suggest that we not only are animals who make and tell narratives but also animals who are told and made by our narratives. The stories we tell are not mere entertainment. Nor do they simply suggest for us some general sense of our heritage. Our stories fully encompass and define our lives. They situate us in reality itself, by elaborating the contours of fundamental moral order, comprising sacred and profane, in narrative form, and placing us too as actors within the larger drama. Our individual and collective lives come to have meaning and purpose insofar as they join the larger cast of characters enacting, reenacting, and perpetuating the larger narrative. It is by finding ourselves placed within a particular drama that we come to know our role, our part, our lines in life—how we are to act, why, and what meaning that has in a larger scheme of reality.

Seeing the connections between narrative, the sacred, culture, and identity helps to make clear why and how human animals mark time together. Humans are not content simply to let the earth revolve around the sun from season to season and to carry out their instrumentally functional tasks within seasons. Instead, humans always and everywhere use time to invest time and their lives with meaning through stories. Moral, believing animals recurrently mark time by designating particular dates and seasons that recall what for them is hallowed by invoking and retelling their particular narratives. This is crucial in sustaining the collective identities within which individual identities can be known and lived.

Moral, believing Americans, for example, mark each of the earth's revolutions around the sun with holidays—etymologically, "holy days," not incidentally—that retell our stories about Martin Luther King, Jr.; Abraham Lincoln; George Washington; American soldiers who have fought and died; the Declaration of Independence from Britain; the laborers who built our economy; Christopher Columbus; the first Thanksgiving; Pearl Harbor; and Christmas. Diverse American subcultures also overlay these holy days by marking time in celebrating—etymologically, "solemnizing"—Saint Patrick, Passover, Palm Sunday, Good Friday, Easter, Holocaust Remembrance, Rosh Hashanah, Yom Kippur, Halloween, Diwali, All Saint's Day, Hanukkah, Ramadan, Advent, and so on.

What is obvious is that these national holy days do not center on abstract concepts or propositional arguments. They all center on and recall narratives, told and retold stories about the struggle for civil rights, Washington chopping down a cherry tree and not lying to his father about it, Lincoln and slavery and the Union, the Revolution, celebrating the New World's harvest bounty with Indians, our entry into World War II, and so on. The stories are not mere excuses for getting time away from work. The stories define who we as a people are, what we are here for, how we ought to live, what we ought to feel, what is good and bad, right and wrong, just and unjust, worthy and unworthy, sacred and profane. This is not only true of Americans. All humans everywhere—from the Shia Muslims in the Near East to the natives of Tahiti to Inuits in the Arctic— do the same thing in their particular ways. (The cynic might say that few of these holidays mean very little to him or her and many others; I would suggest they seriously propose national legislation to wipe these holidays off the calendar and replace them with generic days off from work every three weeks, and see what kind of reception that evokes.)

To some degree, the centrality of narrative throws a different light on our theories of culture. Older anthropological theories, for instance, tended to speak of culture as sum total collections of learned knowledge and human artifacts that people needed to master to function in society. Thus Edward Tylor wrote in 1871 that culture is "that complex whole which includes knowledge, beliefs, art, morals, law, custom, and any other capabilities and habits acquired by man as a member of society."[11] Sort of an all-this-and-the-kitchen-sink approach. But recognizing the ordering role of narrative in culture helps to bring some coherence to this list of items; it helps us to see some of the connections and patterns across and within these cultural elements. To some extent, the norms, values, beliefs, symbols, laws, customs, and so on are not simply a jumble of discreet elements in a cultural grab bag. Many of them are at least loosely linked together in some meaningful way by the particular narratives that orient and direct the culture or subculture.

11. Edward Tylor, *Primitive Culture* (New York: Harper and Row, 1958 [1871]).

A similar argument applies to some more recent theories, such as Ann Swidler's "Culture in Action" theory, discussed hereafter, which employs the cultural "toolkit" metaphor.[12] The idea of cultural tools nicely highlights the potential of strategies of action to be put to use to achieve various purposes. What the image tends to obscure, however, is the essential narrative constitution and ordering of culture. Tools are mere practical instruments for manipulating the physical world. Cultures, however, are epics, dramas, parables, legends, allegories. The meanings and motivations of culture are matters not finally of practical accomplishment but emplotted moral significance.

More generally, this book has argued that human culture and motivation to action are not at bottom instrumentally functional or practically rational matters but rather are very much normative concerns. It is orientation to moral order, I have suggested, and not innate acquisitiveness or functional practicality that most powerfully moves and guides human action. If it were otherwise, as Marshall Sahlins has suggested, then Americans would eat dogs as readily as they eat cows—as some cultures indeed do. Dog meat is, after all, nutritious and could be produced for market quite economically—especially if dog pounds and animal shelters proved cooperative. But, as Marshall Sahlins astutely notes, "America is the land of the sacred dog," so we can never even consider eating dog. The very thought cannot stand in our minds. Eating dog is taboo, a violation of something sacred in our moral order. Still, this chapter does part ways with Sahlins in suggesting that the organizing principles behind the normative orders of culture are openly narrative in form, more contingent, and not rooted in some deep, complex cognitive structure, as Sahlins, if I understand him correctly, would seem to have it (and that it is the structural anthropologist's job to uncover). Cultures and motivations are not random, arbitrary, inexplicable jumbles of categories and ideas, not even assorted collections of cultural tools in toolkits. Yet that is not because of the ordering power of some given "deep structure" but rather because culture and motivation are generated and sustained by various

12. Ann Swidler, "Culture in Action: Symbols and Strategies," *American Sociological Review* 51 (1986): 273–86; also see Claude Lévi-Strauss, *The Savage Mind* (Chicago: University of Chicago Press, 1966), 17–18.

narrative constitutions of what for moral, believing animals is real, significant, and good. The normative is thus organized by the narrative.

The most fundamental point here is this: narrative is our most elemental human genre of communication and meaning-making, an essential way of framing the order and purpose of reality, that we moderns need and use every bit as much as our primitive ancestors. Most other forms of abstract, rational, analytical discourse are always rooted in, contextualized by, and significant because of the underlying stories that narrate our lives. If so, then scholarly disciplines that study human life, such as sociology, will most fundamentally need to engage in practices that are closer to the work of literary interpretation than mathematical prediction—whatever loss of scientific status that may involve.[13]

The Narratives of American Sociology

The discipline of American sociology itself provides an example of the ways big stories actually undergird and make important human practices that themselves appear on the surface to be unrelated to the mythical constitution of reality. Mainstream sociology understands itself to be a kind of science of human social life. It employs rational, systematic methods of empirical data collection and hypothesis testing to make valid and reliable claims about social facts, processes, relationships, and structures. Sociology is concerned to minimize biases in sampling and observation, to replicate findings, to build bodies of generalizable theory, to describe and analyze human social behaviors and practices in ways undistorted by the potential interests and prejudices of the sociologist's particularistic ideology or tradition—perhaps even to be "objective." This is the sociological center, around which also encamp a variety of more "critical,"

13. Craig Calhoun rightly observes: "There may . . . [be] deeper reasons for [the] sociological avoidance of the study of culture. To take culture very seriously might [mean] an implicit challenge to the positivist self-understanding and the dominance of objectivist research techniques in sociology." Craig Calhoun, "Introduction: Social Issues in the Study of Culture," *Comparative Social Research* 11 (1989): 2.

"interpretive," and feminist schools of sociology, which in different ways claim to contest some of these features of the mainstream.

But what most if not all of these versions of American sociology have in common—however scientistic versus "critical" they may be—is that they are ultimately animated, energized, and made significant by one of two historical narrative traditions. Apart from these two narrative traditions, sociology itself would hold little human interest to anyone. Why should any but a few technical experts care about significance tests, fieldnotes, network structures, oversampling techniques, or interaction effects? It all means nothing without a larger context and purpose, neither of which sociology itself could possibly supply. Instead, if and when sociological work is compelling, it is usually because sociology is being carried along by one of two extrascientific narratives—one an optimistic, mobilizing story; the other a fairly cynical, unmasking story. The first I will call the narrative of *Liberal Progress*, the second of *Ubiquitous Egoism;* the former narrates reality roughly as follows.

> Once upon a time, the vast majority of human persons suffered in societies and social institutions that were unjust, unhealthy, repressive, and oppressive. These traditional societies were reprehensible because of their deep-rooted inequality, exploitation, and irrational traditionalism—all of which made life very unfair, unpleasant, and short. But the noble human aspiration for autonomy, equality, and prosperity struggled mightily against the forces of misery and oppression, and eventually succeeded in establishing modern, liberal, democratic, capitalist, welfare societies. While modern social conditions hold the potential to maximize the individual freedom and pleasure of all, there is much work to be done to dismantle the powerful vestiges of inequality, exploitation, and repression. This struggle for the good society in which individuals are equal and free to pursue their self-defined happiness is the one mission truly worth dedicating one's life to achieving.

For sociologists whose scholarship and teaching is embedded within and offered in the service of this liberal progress narrative, the important tasks are clear. Studies in nearly every field of the discipline—but particularly in the areas of social stratification, race and ethnicity, sex and gender, poverty, work and occupations, family, economic sociology—must work to identify privilege, exploitation, prejudice, and unequal opportunity in order to inform cultural practices and policy and legislative reforms that will make society more free, equal, and fulfilling for its individual members. In particular, this means identifying and critiquing class inequality, racism, sexism, heterosexism, corporate exploitation, and other forms of discrimination, privilege, and injustice.

For some sociologists, this struggle takes the form of rigorous quantitative analyses—for example, of the causes of poverty, the dynamics of welfare use, the prevalence of dead-end jobs, the correlates of teenage pregnancy—whose findings speak to politicians, technocrats, and other institutional leaders. In the best case, one's work provides the intellectual backbone of some actual policy initiative, the movement toward which ideally involves an invitation to present one's research findings at a congressional hearing on Capitol Hill. Other versions of sociological scholarship in the service of the liberal progress narrative analyze the historical movement and dynamics of liberal progress itself. These include cross-national research on factors influencing democratization, historical analyses of civil rights movements, comparative studies of international poverty and development, and so on. For yet other, more "critical" sociologists, the liberal progress narrative animates scholarship of a more prophetic style, unmasking and denouncing the racism inherent in the criminal justice system, the sexism embedded in consumer capitalism and patriarchal family structures, the class exploitation of the service economy, the heterosexism pervading routine social practices and legal systems, the militarism entrenched in masculine culture and corporate America, et cetera. Sociologists of this latter style pride themselves for their progressive and radical analyses, said to be more critical and systemic than those their merely liberal, more mainstream colleagues produce. What they seem less aware of, however, is the common underlying liberal progress narrative that animates and makes significant all of these bodies of work as a whole.

But sociology's underlying story is not always about difficult but forward-looking progress and emancipation. Alongside of sociology's primary narrative of liberal progress is its secondary narrative of *Ubiquitous Egoism*, which can be told something like this:

> Once upon a time, people believed that human self-centeredness was a moral flaw needing correction through ethical and spiritual discipline toward self-sacrificial love for neighbor and commitment to the common good. Even today, many people believe this. But as noble as it sounds, more perceptive and honest thinkers have come to see the cold, hard, simple fact

that, beneath all apparent expressions of love and altruism, all human motives and concerns are really self-interested. In fact, notions such as love
and self-sacrifice themselves have been tools of manipulation and advantage
in the hands of Machiavellian actors. Idealists persist in affirming moral
commitment to the welfare of others, but they are naive and misguided.
Truly honest and courageous people who have intellectually "come of age"
are increasingly disabusing themselves of such illusions and learning to be
satisfied with the substitute idealism of helping to build the best society
possible, given the constraints of ubiquitous rational egoism.

Sociologists whose teaching and research is formed by the ubiquitous egoism narrative sometimes tend toward technocratic interests in rational,
quasi-utilitarian institutional reforms and interventions. How, they ask,
can we build better schools and antipoverty programs based on the assumptions of rational egoism? Other sociologists who pursue their scholarly lives within this story play the role of the dramatic unmasker—pro-
phetically exposing the hidden, selfish pleasures and privileges present in
what appear to be activities of love and altruism, such as marriage, family,
and social movement activism. Yet other sociologists in this vein are more
matter-of-fact in their work, detached from the passions of reform and
unmasking, in view of the powerful moral leveling that ubiquitous rational
egoism effects. Their pleasure is simply the interest of the intellectual craft
that sustains their career, particularly in being able to provide unromantic,
comprehensive explanations for all aspects of human social life.

These, then, are the two dominant narratives that ultimately animate
and make meaningful most of the work of contemporary American sociology—however dryly objective and rigorously scientific it may at times
seem to the contrary. Liberal Progress and Ubiquitous Egoism are clearly
distinct in plot and style. The first is an inspiring drama, the second a
more sobering satire. But their differences should not obscure their common source, both deriving from the master narrative of eighteenth- and
nineteenth-century European Enlightenment. One story emphasizes the
emancipatory elements of revolutionary and rationalistic Enlightenment;
the other accentuates aspects of the skeptical and utilitarian streams of
the Enlightenment.[14]

14. Henry May, *The Enlightenment in America* (New York: Oxford University
Press, 1976).

Insofar as the Enlightenment itself was in good measure a renarration of Christianity in secular terms, the two narratives animating contemporary American sociology reflect the optimistic and pessimistic themes that Christianity's theological anthropology united but the Enlightenment split apart. The uncomfortable tension and paradox of the Christian theology of human nature and history have become deeply ingrained in Western culture and consciousness. That is, on the one hand humans are seen as creatures made in the image of God, possessing an almost divine dignity and glory and destined through grace and redemption to flourish in community and love on earth and in heaven. On the other hand and simultaneously, humans are seen as wickedly sinful, suffering the dreadful consequences of self-inflicted depravity and rebellion against God and so inclined toward deep and sustained self-centeredness, pride, alienation, hatred, and self-destruction. This paradox, which orthodox Christianity always held in dynamic tension, the Enlightenment pried apart and stripped of the divine. In the end, the Liberal Progress narrative is a secularized retelling of the righteous half and Ubiquitous Egoism of the other, sinful half. Since the Enlightenment, we in the West no longer have had to live with the complexity and discomfort inherent in the Christian paradoxical view of humanity. We can decide instead simply to be either credulously optimistic or cynically pessimistic.[15] Either way, sociology provides an attractive academic means through which to live out those narratives.

It may be worth noting that in previous decades sociology also comprised a third narrative tradition that animated significant work in the discipline. This third story was rooted in German and English Romanticism, which was itself a reaction against the rationalism and skepticism of the Enlightenment. We might call it the *Community Lost narrative* and retell it like this:

> Once upon a time, folk lived together in local, face-to-face communities where we knew and took care of each other. Life was simple and sometimes hard. But we lived in harmony with nature, laboring honestly at the plough and in handcraft. Life was securely woven in homespun fabrics of organic,

15. Here I follow the basic argument of Reinhold Niebuhr's Gifford Lectures, published as *The Nature and Destiny of Man* (New York: Charles Scribner's Sons, 1948).

integrated culture, faith, and tradition. We truly knew who we were and felt deeply for our land, our kin, our customs. But then a dreadful thing happened. Folk community was overrun by the barbarisms of modern industry, urbanization, rationality, science, fragmentation, anonymity, transience, and mass production. Faith began to erode, social trust dissipate, folk customs vanish. Work became alienating, authentic feeling repressed, neighbors strangers, and life standardized and rationalized. Those who knew the worth of simplicity, authentic feeling, nature, and custom resisted the vulgarities and uniformities of modernity. But all that remains today are tattered vestiges of a world we have lost. The task of those who see clearly now is to memorialize and celebrate folk community, mourn its ruin, and resist and denounce the depravities of modern, scientific rationalism that would kill the Human Spirit.

In contrast to the inspiring drama of Liberal Progress and the sobering satire of Ubiquitous Egoism, the Community Lost narrative is a nostalgic tragedy evoking melancholy and dissent for those who have told and lived it. It renarrates in secular terms not the sundered elements of the Christian theology of human nature but the Jewish and Christian story of paradise lost, of original sin, of the serpent in the Garden. Within sociology, the Community Lost story has animated whole schools of social theory and generated entire research programs in urban and community sociology and studies of immigration. It has also provided much of the gut-level appeal of secularization theory in the sociology of religion and sustained some sociological interest in theorizing the arts, particularly in exploring the potential redemptive power of poetry and visual art. One hears strong echoes of Community Lost in the works of Tönnies, Weber, Maine, Simmel, Wirth, Adorno, Marcuse, Nisbet, and others up through the 1970s.

But Community Lost is a narrative that itself has lost much of its appeal to contemporary sociologists since the 1980s. Its tragic, backward-looking romanticism offers much less narrative appeal than sociology's dominant Liberal Progress story, at least in the current social context. It is, after all, much more alluring and meaningful—particularly in a post-Christian culture still haunted with feelings for a redemptive kingdom—to struggle valiantly through one's profession for progressive equality and emancipation than to document and mourn the loss of a harmony, innocence, and authentic feeling that can never be regained. So the Community Lost myth has somewhat receded into the background in sociology. Whether social and cultural disruptions—like those of the Sixties that gave rise to the neoromantic commune and "back to the land" movements of that era (and sociological studies of them)—might revive the Community Lost narrative again among sociologists of the future is an open question. But Community Lost is not one of sociology's dominant myths at the beginning of the twenty-first century.

Whatever the particular narratives are that undergird the sociological enterprise, the more basic point here is that sociologists in their work are no less than other humans the makers, tellers, and believers of narrative construals of existence, history, and purpose. Sociologists not only make stories but are animals who are made by their stories. They also tell and retell myths that themselves come fundamentally to constitute and direct their professional work and, often, their personal lives. They, like all people, most fundamentally understand what reality is, who they are, and how they ought to live by locating themselves within the larger narratives and metanarratives that they hear and tell, which constitute that which is for them real and significant. No one, not even the statistics laden sociologist, escapes the moral, believing, narrative-constituted condition of the human animal.

Where That Leaves Us

The problem with a narratological understanding of human persons—and probably an important reason modern people resist thinking of themselves as ultimately storytelling and believing and incarnating animals—is that it is difficult rationally to adjudicate between divergent stories. How do you tell which one is more deserving of assent and commitment than others? The American Experiment narrative will probably appeal to more readers of this book than the Militant Islamic Resurgence narrative. Why? Because objective, empirical evidence proves that it is a truer story? Not really. For what *is* evidence is *itself* largely made significant, if not constituted for us, by our narratives. Which is why few readers of this book could ever in the short run convince with empirical evidence a militant Muslim to drop his or her mission and believe and live out the American Experiment story instead. Such Muslims' big story makes them read the same "facts" quite differently from most Americans, who simply believe a different story.

Does this mean we must all become relativists, perhaps even tolerant nihilists? Must we throw up our hands and declare that since no story can be truly neutrally evaluated or entirely empirically adjudicated that therefore all stories are equally valid (or invalid)?

First, we simply cannot do that, even if we wanted to. That is an anthropological impossibility. Nobody is really a relativist, no matter what they say. Scratch hard enough—usually it doesn't take much—and one discovers that hard-core "relativists" are in fact believers and actors in some story or other. That is just the kind of animal we are. Nobody can simply exempt himself or herself from the human condition. We must narrate and believe and live out stories, and we *do* narrate and believe and live out stories, inevitably. In the end, it appears, our stories are not so much at the disposal of our lives, as we choose to construct our lives. Rather, our lives are more profoundly constructed by the stories that encompass and compose them. Our lives are only ever meaningful because we know the particular big and small stories into which they fit, even if we are not always aware of that, per se. We ourselves become minor but significant actors in the larger drama, even when the drama seems to us perfectly real. And maybe it is. In this sense, relativism is not an option. It is only an apparent option, which itself could only make sense within a particular life-forming narrative about freedom, choice, and enlightenment. Sartrean existentialism, Enlightenment liberalism, and similar stories thus turn out to be forms of bad faith. Not because we pretend we have no choices when in fact we have many but rather because we pretend we have many choices when in fact we have few. Objective, rational, definitive appraisals of narratives is impossible. But escape from our narrative construals of reality is impossible too. We turn out simply to be more caught, more stuck, more dependent in fact than the modern story of the autonomously choosing self, which we have believed and have tried to live out, could ever let on.

Yet that does not directly answer the question. For our empirical inability to live as relativists does not preclude the theoretical possibility that, in principle, we still possess no capacity to talk across our narratives in ways that might in some meaningful manner adjudicate between them. It is worth realizing that none of us finally are relativists in actuality. But that does not necessarily mean that our actual situation is not a relativistic one in which any discussion between and evaluations of different narratives is finally impossible. We *are* committed, moral, believing animals who do not have at our disposal a universal, indubitable foundation of knowledge by which to judge our own and others' beliefs and stories neutrally, objectively, and definitively. So does that mean we must despair of meaningful discussion across human differences, of even trying to offer reasonable accounts for why one life-constituting story may be preferable to another? I think not.

Lived experience provides some starting-point clues here.[16] It is true that people have an immensely difficult, sometimes impossible time convincing each other of the truth of their positions. It is also true that many contemporary moral debates are emotivist and seemingly interminable in character.[17] Yet people nevertheless keep on discussing and arguing and sometimes—often slowly and with great difficulty—actually seem to get somewhere, despite the lack of a universal, indubitable foundation of Truth. Sometimes, though not always, people come better to understand their own and others' views through arguments with rivals. In some cases, people revise their own views because of rivals' challenges. At times, people actually discard their previous commitments, modify their assumptions, and embrace new beliefs. And sometimes people even undergo wholesale conversion to entirely different worldviews. If meaningful discussion, persuasion, and adjudication between different presuppositions and narratives was literally impossible, none of these things could happen. Nor would my writing and your reading this book (and very many other books) itself be anything but a complete waste of time. For, precisely *because of* my own particularistic commitments, I write this book as an attempt to challenge the assumptions and commitments of rival approaches to social theory to try to persuade readers to embrace the alternative perspective advanced here. These observations together suggest that we do possess at least some ways partially to adjudicate between rival presuppositions and narratives in some cases, at least, even if never with

16. Here I follow Charles Taylor on the value of attending to intractable human experience, in *Sources of the Self* (Cambridge: Harvard University Press, 1989), 3–8.

17. MacIntyre, *After Virtue*.

certainty or from a neutral or objective standpoint. Rivals in fact do find persuasive things to say to each other, even about their basic assumptions and dearest stories, and on that basis they sometimes alter their views and commitments.

It is beyond the scope of this book to elaborate theoretically how, why, and when rival presuppositions and narratives might be engaged and judged. But it is worth briefly noting what are at least some efforts in different fields to undertake just that project. In the field of moral philosophy, for example, Jeffrey Stout has elaborated an approach to meaningful moral deliberation in a morally pluralistic situation, arguing that "the facts of moral diversity don't compel us to become nihilists or skeptics, to abandon the notions or moral truth and justified moral belief." According to Stout, it is difficult, but not impossible, to find a middle ground between the extremes of "complete loss of confidence" and "aspiration to a God's-eye view" when it comes to moral truth, and his book suggests ways to help find that middle ground.[18] Alasdair MacIntyre, working with a tradition-centered epistemology, suggests means by which traditions may engage and evaluate each other: "Is there any way in which one of these rivals might prevail over the others? One possible answer was supplied by Dante: that narrative prevails over its rivals which is able to include its rivals within it, not only to retell their stories as episodes within its story, but to tell the story of the telling of their stories as such episodes."[19] In the philosophy of science, Roy Bhaskar and colleagues have developed a philosophy of "critical realism" that affirms the existence of a real, common, external reality that observers can actually study and know, even given the influences of their own particularistic human perceptions and commitments; thus human understandings of the world are not wholly constructed in terms of the influences of particular human perceptions and interpretations but rather have some capacity to commonly access an external reality that itself can substantively inform com-

18. Jeffrey Stout, *Ethics After Babel: The Languages of Morals and Their Discontents* (Boston: Beacon Press, 1988), 3, 14.

19. Alasdair MacIntyre, *Three Rival Versions of Moral Enquiry: Encyclopaedia, Genealogy, and Tradition* (Notre Dame, Ind.: University of Notre Dame Press, 1990), 81. Also see Alasdair MacIntyre, 1989. *Whose Justice? Which Rationality?* (Notre Dame, Ind.: University of Notre Dame Press, 1989).

mon understanding.[20] Likewise, Imre Lakatos has sought to develop an understanding of knowledge that discards positivist assumptions and recognizes human and historical aspects of scientific inquiry yet does not accede to antirealism. Lakatos pursues this by reformulating Kuhn's concept of incommensurate paradigms into the idea of a "methodology of scientific research program" that denies the incommensurability of large-scale theories, thus defending the rationality of theory change among scientists.[21] The philosopher of science Larry Laudan has advanced a similar kind of argument.[22] Even in the 1940s, 1950s, and 1960s, chemist turned philosopher of science Michael Polanyi was similarly exploring compelling ways that scholars might reasonably adjudicate between competing theoretical frameworks of knowledge while taking very seriously the personal, tacit, and faith-like character of scientific knowing.[23]

20. Roy Bhaskar, *A Realist Theory of Science* (Sussex: Harvester Press, 1978); *Scientific Realism and Human Emancipation* (London: Verso, 1986); *Reclaiming Reality: A Critical Introduction to Contemporary Philosophy* (London: Verso, 1989). Also see Rom Harré, *On Social Being* (Oxford: Basil Blackwell, 1979); Andrew Collier, *Critical Realism* (London: Verso, 1989); Margaret Archer, *Being Human: The Problem of Agency* (Cambridge: Cambridge University Press, 2000); Mats Ekström, "Causal Explanation and Social Action: The Contribution of Max Weber and of Critical Realism to a Generative View of Causal Explanation in Social Science," *Acta Sociologica* 35 (1992): 107–22; Tony Lawson, "A Realist Theory for Economics," in Roger Backhouse (ed.), *New Directions in Economic Methodology* (New York: Routledge, 1994).

21. Imre Lakatos, *The Methodology of Scientific Research Programmes: Philosophical Papers, Volume 1*, ed. John Worrall and Gregory Currie (Cambridge: Cambridge University Press, 1978). Also see Sergio Sismondo, *Science without Myth: On Construction, Reality, and Social Knowledge* (Albany: State University of New York Press, 1996).

22. Larry Laudan, *Progress and Its Problems: Toward a Theory of Scientific Growth* (Berkeley: University of California Press, 1977); *Science and Relativism: Some Key Controversies in the Philosophy of Science* (Chicago: University of Chicago Press, 1990); *Beyond Positivism and Relativism: Theory, Method, and Evidence* (Boulder, Colo.: Westview Press, 1996).

23. Michael Polanyi, *Science, Faith, and Society* (Chicago: University of Chicago Press, 1946); *Personal Knowledge: Toward a Post-Critical Philosophy* (Chicago: University of Chicago Press, 1958); *The Tacit Dimension* (New York: Doubleday, 1966).

The point here is not that any of these authors have definitively answered the question and settled the matter. The point, rather, is that the discussion does not end with Kuhn and Feyerabend, or with Stanley Fish or Richard Rorty,[24] for that matter. The positivist program is philosophically dead. The strong foundationalism that underwrote a supposedly universal rationality that definitively adjudicated between human differences is dead. But this does not necessarily throw us into the tribal power struggles of utter relativism. The narratological and presuppositionalist views advanced here do not necessarily lead to the kinds of antirealism, skepticism, or nihilism that end meaningful debates across human presuppositions and stories. Instead, it helps us to own up to some of the reasons why those debates are so difficult, and to learn to carry on those debates in ways more appropriate to our condition as moral, believing animals.

Shifting focus somewhat, practically speaking, more important than the issue of adjudicating between rival narratives is the problem of learning how to live with each other, how to deliberate civilly about our common human life together, given that we often do live, move, and have our being within different narratives. Note that this issue is not important to everyone and for all narratives, but it most likely will be to most readers of this book and certainly is to its author. Thus the challenge for moral, believing animals on this earth is finally not how to work out which among ours is the one true story but rather and more immediately figuring out how to talk and live together, given the fact of our different stories. This is the challenge of civil pluralism. Given what this and previous chapters have argued, this can only be possible not because a universally shared Reason underlies all of our narratives but rather because many particularistic narratives contain within themselves the resources for living civilly with difference. Both Christianity and Islam, for example, are

24. Stanley Fish, *Is There a Text in This Class?: The Authority of Interpreting Communities* (Cambridge: Harvard University Press, 1980); *There's No Such Thing as Free Speech, and It's a Good Thing Too* (New York: Oxford University Press, 1994); "Why Can't We All Just Get Along?" *First Things* 60 (1996): 18–27; Richard Rorty, *Philosophy and the Mirror of Nature* (Princeton, N.J.: Princeton University Press, 1979); Rorty, *Consequences of Pragmatism* (Minneapolis: University of Minnesota Press, 1982).

narratives that do make absolute and universal claims and have well-known histories—as do many other traditions—of persecuting difference. But Christianity and Islam also equally possess their own internal theological resources with which to live civilly with real difference. All of the same might be said of many other religious and secular narratives. Thus confronting the inescapably enstoried nature of our lives does not have to lead to violent and oppressive tribal power struggles of utter relativism. While fully living within our truly different narratives, we might still draw on our narratives to learn to live together in some measure of peace.

In any case, to whatever extent and in whatever ways we are able to adjudicate between and live with our differing, constituting presuppositions and narratives, we can and should at least *be aware* of our stories, and of ourselves as animals who make and are made by our stories. And when we moderns tell our stories about how we have evolved beyond our primitive storytelling ancestors, we can, with some honesty, at least wink and nod about the irony of it all. Some may have succumbed to the particular modern story about the absolute chance and purposelessness of everything, which Bertrand Russell summed up nicely at the start of the twentieth century with this faith-based quasi-narrative:

> That man is the product of causes which had no prevision of the end they were achieving; that his origin, his growth, his hopes and fears, his loves and his beliefs are but the outcome of accidental collocations of atoms; that no fire, no heroism, no intensity of thought and feeling, can preserve an individual life beyond the grave; that all the labors of the ages, all the devotion, all the inspiration, all the noonday brightness of human genius, are destined to extinction in the vast death of the solar system, and that the whole temple of man's achievements must inevitably be buried beneath the debris of a universe in ruins—all these things, if not quite beyond dispute, are yet so nearly certain that no philosophy which rejects them can hope to stand. Only within the scaffolding of these truths, only on the firm foundation of unyielding despair, can the soul's habitation henceforth be safely built.[25]

25. Bertrand Russell, *Mysticism and Logic* (New York: Barnes and Noble, 1917), 47–48. Note even Russell's desire here to hold on to *truth* in face of the alleged utter purposelessness of and despair over life.

But for those of us who have not succumbed to this story, we may hold out some hope, perhaps even the conviction, that life and the cosmos really are significant, that in the fabric of reality there really is out there The Story, of which some of our stories are but telling echoes.

FIVE

ON RELIGION

What is religion? And why are so many people in the world religious? These are old questions, in answer to which much ink has been spilled in recent centuries. To some extent they are simply impossible questions, incapable of being answered satisfactorily. For quite a while now, many scholars have been weary of the "definition of religion" debate. And even more scholars have simply jettisoned the "origins of religion" question. It has all come to seem so antiquated, so futile.

Yet religion is simply too fascinating a thing to let sit, to not continue to probe fundamental questions about it. We pretty well know what people are up to, and why, when they labor to produce goods and services for consumption. We know why people engage in political life to make collective decisions. We know why they build armies, form families, write laws, and educate youth.

But why do people, very many people, engage in religion? Why do they take seriously realities that are unseen? What induces people to give away time and money and perhaps much more for intangible things "spiritual"? What are people doing when they pray, and why are they doing it? What is it that gets people out of bed every Sunday morning for their entire lives? Or to abstain from food and sex during daylight hours for an entire month every year? Nobody is finally making people do religion. It does not produce any obvious material benefit. In much of the world, religion is entirely voluntary. In other parts of the world it is actively suppressed. And yet billions of humans profess and practice religion anyway. What an interesting phenomenon.

Not only that, but religion—this thing apparently based finally on nothing empirical—actually seems very often significantly to influence people's lives in various ways. It can really matter in real outcomes in life. Studies of religion are recurrently discovering that religion often affects people's health, beliefs, attitudes, practices, affiliations, and behaviors. Religion actually appears to cause things to happen.

What is going on here? What is this thing "religion"? Why does it engage people so? What role does it play in human existence? How do we explain its influence in life?

What Is Religion?

The definition-of-religion question has frustrated many scholars because of the recurrent problems of categorizing and of drawing boundaries around "religion" that it inevitably raises. Is Confucianism a religion? Is nontheistic Buddhism a religion? Is Scientology a religion? Is Marxism a religion? Is the Carolina-Duke basketball rivalry a religion? Is religion defined by the substance of things supernatural or divine? Or by the particular social functions it supposedly serves?[1]

We can help to deescalate this line of impossible questioning somewhat by not thinking about religion in essentialist terms, as if we were positivist scientists discovering the natural laws of Religion. Instead we should approach things "religious" as historically and culturally particularistic narratives, beliefs, experiences, practices, and traditions that are interesting and important and need interpreting in their own right. There is no one thing out there, "religion," in any general sense. The specific "things" we call "religions" are not mere instances of some larger, universal property of social reality, Religion. It does appear that human communities have since their beginnings engaged in various practices that we now normally

1. Danièle Hervieu-Léger has written a very interesting (yet in my view ultimately unsatisfying) recent inquiry into conceptualizations of religion in her *Religion as a Chain of Memory* (New Brunswick, N.J.: Rutgers University Press, 2000).

call religious, but that does not mean that there is some standard social property, Religion, the social equivalent to an element on chemistry's periodic table, that the investigator identifies and researches. Indeed, many scholars claim that the idea of "religion" itself as a general human experience and practice is the conceptual invention of certain Western thinkers in the sixteenth through nineteenth centuries who were trying to come to terms intellectually—including theologically—with a wildly diverse, non-Christian, global cultural reality then being discovered through exploration, trade, and colonialization.[2]

Furthermore, it is helpful to remind ourselves that as inquirers we can never investigate religion from a neutral and generic perspective, or even think and talk about religion using neutral and generic "Language." Rather, we necessarily approach things religious specifically as secularists, Roman Catholics, Buddhists, and so on who have been socialized either in the United States, India, or elsewhere and who think and speak not in "Language" but in English or some other particular native tongue. And all of those particularities inevitably shape how we can and do think about religion, including ways that it might be useful for us to define religion.

Having said that, I do not think it would be a constructive move for social scientists to abandon the concept of "religion" altogether. For we do find what appear to be certain common features across the kind of narratives, beliefs, experiences, practices, and traditions that we commonly call "religious," and we can and do find it analytically useful to categorize

2. See, for example, Jonathan Z. Smith, "Religion, Religions, Religious," in Mark C. Taylor (ed.), *Critical Terms in Religious Studies* (Chicago: University of Chicago Press, 1998), 269–84; Talal Asad, *Genealogies of Religion* (Baltimore: Johns Hopkins University Press, 1993); Gustaaf Houtman, "How a Foreigner Invented 'Buddhendom,' " *Journal for the Anthropological Society of Oxford* 21 (1990): 113–28; S. N. Balagangadhara, *"The Heathen in His Blindness": Asia, the West, and the Dynamics of Religion* (Leiden: E. J. Brill, 1994); David Pailin, *Attitudes to Other Religions: Comparative Religion in Seventeenth- and Eighteenth-Century England* (Manchester: Manchester University Press, 1984); Philip Almond, *The British Discovery of Buddhism* (Cambridge: Cambridge University Press, 1988); Lionel Jensen, *Manufacturing "Confucianism": Chinese and Western Imaginings in the Making of a Tradition* (Durham, N.C.: Duke University Press, 1995); Murray Wax, "Religion as Universal: Tribulations of an Anthropological Enterprise," *Zygon* 19 (1984): 5–20.

them together under this single concept.[3] But what is it that religions share in common, or at least that we commonly think of them as sharing in common? What in our thinking and speech sets apart things religious from other social practices and institutions? I think it is most helpful to think about religions in this way: *religions are sets of beliefs, symbols, and practices about the reality of superempirical orders that make claims to organize and guide human life.*[4] Put more simply, if less precisely, what we mean by religion is an ordinarily unseen reality that tells us what truly is and how we therefore ought to live.

This idea needs some unpacking. First, religion for us concerns a "superempirical order," an ordered reality that is not normally observable with the five human senses. Religion affirms that such an order is real and consequential, even though it normally cannot be directly seen, heard, touched, smelled, or tasted. Second, this approach intentionally emphasizes the "superempirical" rather than the more commonly referenced "supernatural." This is because supernatural implies that the unseen order, the "spiritual," is not a part of nature, and that nature consists only of physical matter. Yet some religions understand the unseen order as very much part of nature, a reality inhering in the world or cosmos; some religions also understand nature, the world, the cosmos to be a whole reality comprising both the empirical and superempirical together.[5] Third,

3. Donald Brown, *Human Universals* (New York: McGraw-Hill, 1991), 139. At the very least, we should be able to formulate a nominal and particularistic definition of religion that keys on common term usage, instead of a realist definition seeking to demarcate what out there is truly religious from nonreligious. On this, and the point above about not speaking "Language," see John Sommerville, "Resurrecting Religion in a New (Hermeneutical) Dimension," *Fides et Historia* 30 (1998): 20–31.

4. In this and the next paragraph, I closely follow the argument of George Thomas, "Religions Engage Everyday Life" (unpublished manuscript, Department of Sociology, Arizona State University, 2001). Thomas himself follows, though revises, Roland Robertson, who described religion as "that set of beliefs and symbols (and values derived directly therefrom) pertaining to a distinction between an empirical and a superempirical, transcendent reality; the affairs of the empirical being subordinated in significance to the nonempirical." Roland Robertson, *The Sociological Interpretation of Religion* (Oxford: Basil Blackwell, 1970), 47.

5. This approach also avoids using the concept "transcendent" (in Robertson's definition in the previous footnote), since, as Thomas explains, "In many religions

distinguishing the empirical from the superempirical in this way does not mean that the empirical cannot represent or communicate about the superempirical. The distinction is not absolute nor unbridgeable. Indeed, humans, as embodied, sensory animals, normally come to learn about and relate to superempirical orders at least in part precisely through empirical means—through texts read, narratives heard, chants sung, bread and wine tasted, icons beheld, water and ashes touched, suffering endured, and so on. Furthermore, most if not all religions hold that in particular circumstances the superempirical may be physically seen, smelled, heard, tasted, or felt—through epiphanies, visions, angelic appearances, miracles, incarnations, ecstatic experiences, demonic possessions, and so on—which many people historically and alive today profess to have witnessed.[6] Fourth, the approach here emphasizes the decidedly normative concern of religion. Religion is not simply about providing humans with information or knowledge but also, viewed sociologically, about the proper organization and right guidance of life. Religion tells people not only what is real but also consequently what are good, right, true, wise, and worthy desires, thoughts, feelings, values, practices, actions, and interactions. Religion tells us what for us ought to be, in light of the superempirical

---

(e.g., Hinduism) the superempirical is not transcendent (above and distinct from the empirical) but rather immanent (hidden in the empirical)." Thomas, "Religions Engage Everyday Life." Also see J. Milton Yinger, *The Scientific Study of Religion* (New York: Macmillan, 1970), 15–16.

6. See, for example, Christian Smith, Michael Emerson, Sally Gallagher, Paul Kennedy, and David Sikkink, *American Evangelicalism: Embattled and Thriving* (Chicago: University of Chicago Press, 1998), 173–77; M. Scott Peck, *People of the Lie* (New York: Simon and Schuster), 182–211; Kenneth Woodward, *The Book of Miracles* (New York: Simon and Schuster, 2000); Ronald Finacane, *Miracles and Pilgrims: Popular Beliefs in Medieval England* (Totowa, N.J.: Rowman and Littlefield, 1977); Anthony Finlay, *Demons* (London: Blanford, 1999); John Warwick Montgomery (ed.), *Demon Possession* (Minneapolis: Bethany House, 1976); Jess Bryon Hollenback, *Mysticism* (University Park: Pennsylvania State University Press, 1996); D. Scott Rogo, *Miracles* (New York: Dial Press, 1982); Ben-Ami Scharfstein, *Mystical Experience* (New York: Bobbs-Merrill, 1973). According to a 2000 *Newsweek* poll, 48 percent of Americans report that they have personally experienced or witnessed a miracle (see Woodward, *The Book for of Miracles*). "What Miracles Mean," *Newsweek* 135 (May 1, 2000): 54–60.

reality that is. William James suggested this very point in saying that "the life of religion . . . consists of the belief that there is an unseen order, and that our supreme good lies in harmoniously adjusting ourselves thereto."[7]

If this is what religion is to us, then what is nonreligious or secular? These may mean the conscious denial that any superempirical order actually exists—the corollary to the positive affirmation that the only and total reality that actually exists is that which humans can empirically observe on a regular basis ("There is no God; existence is nothing but the natural operation of energy and matter"). Or these may mean that people simply have never seriously considered whether or not a superempirical reality exists, because they have been socialized in an areligious or antireligious context (such as parts of communist China or Soviet Russia). Or these may mean a passive belief that a superempirical reality may exist but a fundamental indifference to the normative claims that the superempirical order makes about the proper organization and guidance of life ("Sure I believe in God, who don't? But that don't make much difference how I live one way or the other").

Note, however, that to be nonreligious or secular does *not* mean that one is not a believer, that one does not continually place one's faith in premises, assumptions, and suppositions that cannot be objectively substantiated or justified without recourse to other believed-in premises, assumptions, and presuppositions. Everyone—the secularist and nonreligious included—is a believing animal, ultimately a person of faith (as I contended in chapter 3). Indeed, the belief that the only and total reality that actually exists is that which humans can empirically observe is itself a statement of faith, whether or not its adherents recognize and admit it as such. Note, too, that to be nonreligious or secular does *not* mean that

---

7. William James, *The Varieties of Religious Experience* (New York: Touchstone, 1997 [1901–2]), 59. James's focus on an "unseen order" comports with the approach of this chapter, although nearly all of the rest of his book focuses instead, and much less helpfully, I think, on subjective individual experience, and not an unseen ordered reality, as the basis of religion. To be clear, furthermore, I do not mean the emphasis on the moral here to reduce religion to mere ethical systems, as strains of liberal Protestantism have often done. By moral, I mean something much bigger and thicker than mere ethical teachings.

one's life is not fundamentally organized and guided by a larger moral order above and beyond oneself. Everyone—religious and secular alike— is a moral animal, is constituted, motivated, and governed by the moral order(s) existing inside and outside of themselves (as I contended in chapter 2). What distinguishes religious people from nonreligious and secular people, therefore, is not that the former are moral, believing animals while the latter are not. What distinguishes them is that the former significantly believe in and are governed by moral order(s) grounded in some super- empirical reality, while the latter believe in and are governed by moral order(s) grounded in some ordering reality that is not superempirical but immanent (or at least that they presume to be so).[8] All humans are thus, at bottom, really quite similar in most of these respects. Where they differ tremendously is in the particular cultural moral orders to which they commit their lives.

Even so, it is worth recognizing that religion can—though it not always necessarily does—profoundly influence the lives of nonreligious and sec- ular people. Precisely because all moral orders are *orders*, and not simply individual ideas or preferences, those moral orders that are grounded in superempirical realities can very well organize and govern the lives of people who do not as individuals espouse any belief in superempirical reality. It can do this in one or both of two ways, internally or externally. Religion can influence the lives of nonreligious people "internally" by forming in their subjective (mental, emotional, volitional) selves moral perceptions, dispositions, values, and commitments that in fact have def- inite religious sources but that the individual cannot or does not con- sciously justify by appeal to those sources. In such cases, it is often difficult to sort out accounts of sources and justifications. But, for example, when an agnostic who was raised a devout Methodist so happens to rest every single Sunday and feels vaguely guilty (not just annoyed) when he has to work on Sundays, the old religious moral order that once shaped his self is still operative within him. And when the Roman Catholic who has unhappily left the Church and thinks of herself as a moral relativist of sorts nevertheless finds herself opposing abortion, the death penalty, and

8. Which, again, may be distinguished from immanent religions, in which the superempirical reality is not transcendent, but immanent, hiddenly present in the empirical.

euthanasia, it is likely that she has not left elements of her former faith far behind.

Religion can also influence the lives of nonreligious people "externally," by historically forming social institutions that create social roles, opportunities, and constraints that affect people's actions and outcomes, whether the institutions continue to do so with reference to the religious justifications that historically generated them, or not. Again, attributing such causal formations and influences is tricky. But, for instance, when American gays and lesbians find it difficult to secure recognized civil unions and the accompanying insurance benefits enjoyed by married heterosexuals, significant outcomes in their lives are in fact being influenced by historical and perhaps current religious beliefs and interests—whatever anyone's own religious commitments may or many not be. Likewise, when Americans of any religious conviction find themselves the beneficiaries (or victims) of innumerable hospitals, colleges, orphanages, and other voluntary and reform organizations that were begun by religious activists in the wake of historical revivals and awakenings, their lives are still being affected by religiously grounded moral orders that have reached into the future. In fact, many social institutions that serve various publics have religious origins, regardless of how secularized they have since become, including the United Way, Habitat for Humanity, Amnesty International, the Salvation Army, Oxfam International, the YMCA, Peace Brigades International, and Greenpeace.[9]

Often such internal and external religious influences combine in interesting ways. Thanksgiving, for instance, is no doubt celebrated by as high a proportion of nonreligious as religious Americans, although its historical reference is religious—the Pilgrims wanted to give thanks to

9. Jackie Smith, Ron Pagnucco, and Winnie Romeril, "Transnational Social Movement Organizations in the Global Political Arena," *Voluntas* 5, no. 2 (1994): 121–54; Lowell Livezey, "U.S. Religious Organizations and the International Human Rights Movement," *Human Rights Quarterly* 11 (1989): 14–81; Alvin Schmidt, *Under the Influence: How Christianity Transformed Civilization* (Grand Rapids, Mich.: Zondervan, 2001). For a more general treatment of this theme, see William Clebsch, *From Sacred to Profane America: The Role of Religion in American History* (New York: Harper and Row, 1968); also see Willis Glover, *Biblical Origins of Modern Secular Culture* (Macon, Ga.: Mercer University Press, 1984).

their God for his blessings on their venture in the New World. As an "external" religious influence, in this sense, Thanksgiving has become (since the nineteenth century) a veritable institution that compels people's participation and celebration. "Internally," millions of nonreligious Americans genuinely feel some significant sense on this holiday of being thankful for the good things in their lives. Thankful *to whom* exactly is not clear, but thankful nonetheless. In any case, if it were not for the theistic Pilgrims who did have someone to whom to be thankful, and nineteenth-century activists to memorialize it, none of us would be taking the time to be with family, eat turkey, watch football, and reflect with thankfulness on our lives.

These influencing processes can, of course, work in the opposite direction. The normative imperatives of nonreligious moral orders may also internally form the subjective selves and externally shape the institutionally governed practices of religious believers. Since few, if any, religious believers live in fully encapsulated, "total" religious worlds—even the Amish have to sell and buy some produce and products—we should expect this nonreligious influencing of religious believers to be significant, perhaps extensive. To what extent this is a problem for religious communities depends on the degree to which the influencing nonreligious moral order is a competitor of or antithetical to the religious moral order. When an American Catholic imbibes capitalism's rational risk management by purchasing costly life insurance (rather than, say, simply trusting the future to God and the Church), it is not too difficult for her to reconcile that action with the moral order of her faith. It becomes more difficult when the same American Catholic becomes influenced by (what some observe to be) America's pervasive "divorce culture" and divorces her infuriatingly self-centered husband; or agrees under advice from doctors, insurers, and "ethics boards" to withdraw life support from her brain-damaged child. And when this American Catholic woman decides not to divorce her husband (in the short run) but instead decides that together they should join their city's polyamorous swingers club and explore all manner of sensual experimentation with a variety of others, this nonreligious moral influence on her life has indeed become quite a problem for her religious community. Of course, drawing and maintaining or renegotiating such boundaries is a continual challenge for religious communities, particularly those that do not culturally and institutionally dominate the larger social order. This is precisely what generates so much discussion and conflict in religious communities.

Understanding religions in this way—as superempirically referenced wellsprings of moral order—helps to explain both how secularization can happen, and why secularization will probably never get very far. All humans are moral, believing animals who must be embedded within and acting out moral order, simply to be human. However, those moral orders need not be directly grounded on superempirical reality but may rather be ones with strictly empirical references. Typical candidates here include secularized liberal, democratic capitalism; Marxist communism; nonreligious expressive, Romantic individualism; and cynical nihilism. And because humans are fairly adaptable creatures culturally, at least in the short run, they can live within and act out such nonreligious moral orders quite functionally. As nonreligious moral orders displace religious moral orders—either internally, externally, or both—the world becomes more secularized. Instances of this are well known.[10]

But lo and behold, it seems that many human animals are recurrently attracted to superempirically grounded moral orders. The exact reasons for this recurrent attraction no doubt vary by time and place, but they appear to include some of the following. Compared to immanently grounded, secular moral orders, many superempirically grounded ones often carry much more weight and authority as long, historical traditions; they seem to provide "deeper roots" than many nonreligious alternatives.[11] Moreover, religious moral orders seem to answer certain recurrently pressing, core existential questions better than nonreligious ones do. How should one meet death? What is the meaning of tragedy? What is the significance of love? What is the basis of obligation?[12] The empirically

10. See, for instance, Christian Smith (ed.), *The Secular Revolution: Power, Conflict, and Interest in the Secularization of American Public Life* (Berkeley: University of California Press, 2003); Steve Bruce, "Christianity in Britain, R.I.P.," *Sociology of Religion* 62, no. 2 (2001): 191–203. Also see Mark Chaves, "Secularization as Declining Religious Authority," *Social Forces* 72, no. 3 (1994): 749–75.

11. See, for example, Lynn Davidman, *Tradition in a Rootless World: Women Turn to Orthodox Judaism* (Berkeley: University of California Press, 1993).

12. Daniel Bell, "The Return of the Sacred?" in *The Winding Passage* (New York: Basic Books, 1980). One nonreligious response is to deny or change the

grounded moral orders of science and socialism and procedural democracy seem limited in their ability to speak profoundly and reassuringly to these questions. Furthermore, the thought that the entire human story is in fact by chance floating around in a cold and empty universe without purpose or significance, to be extinguished in time, and leaving no judgment or care or remembrance whatsoever, is an idea that appears to have limited appeal to most human animals. Whether true or not, ideas, such as that there does exist a personal, loving God who deeply cares for us, or perhaps that a pervasive Supreme Being or Life Force is drawing us and all differences toward eternal unification in peace and harmony, prove much more attractive to most people. And then there is the question of morality itself. What would be the real basis of any morality if it is not grounded in the reality of a superempirical order? How in an objectively meaningless universe can merely humanly constructed, culturally and historically relative beliefs about morality be really and truly morally valid and binding?[13] Moral philosophers, of course, perpetually debate such questions. But the average human person often seems to find it hard to believe that morality could be morality if it were not rooted in an order that transcends the contingencies of our experiences and constructions. For these and probably many other reasons, it appears that moral, believing animals are not likely anytime soon to cease believing in the superempirical orders that ground the narratives, experiences, and practices of religious life.

In summary, religion is not always about belief in the supernatural or only about things considered sacred. The concept of supernatural is too confining. And humans treat many things in life as sacred that are arguably not very religious. Rather, religions are moral orders rooted in beliefs about superempirical realities. Religion is a particular type of human moral order, one conveying a strong sense of being foundational,

---

questions themselves ("Death and tragedy just are, they have no meaning, there is nothing one can do about them"), but this solution appears to hold limited appeal for many.

13. George Mavrodes, "Religion and the Queerness of Morality," in Robert Audi and William Wainwright (eds.), *Rationality, Religious Belief, and Moral Commitment*, 213–26 (Ithaca, N.Y.: Cornell University Press, 1986); Glenn Tinder, "Can We Be Good without God?" *Atlantic Monthly* 264, no. 6 (1989): 55–67.

cosmological, secure. Religions are also normally aspects or components of some larger moral orders, of which they are contributing parts. Why then does religion causally influence human lives in various ways? Because, as I argued in chapter 2, human motivation to action is profoundly morally oriented, directed by the normative imperatives to affirm and enact moral order. Why then does religion not entirely and consistently govern the lives of believers? Because most people live their lives negotiating the demands of multiple religious and nonreligious moral orders—compromising here, synthesizing there, compartmentalizing elsewhere. In such a situation, religion can exert a significant, though not total, influence in human life. Understanding when, under what conditions, and why religion does and does not shape human consciousness and action is thus a major task of the student of religious life.

Religious Origins

But is there any more that may be said about the origins of religion? Early American academic sociologists believed that religion was an expression of primitive fear and ignorance.[14] Many nonreligious people I know today think that religion is ultimately only about life after death, hence, in their minds, finally about fear and ignorance as well. Are these adequate accounts of the sources of religion?

Western scholars have for some centuries debated the origins of religion. The task has proved impossible in historical terms, because evidence about the earliest religions is simply lost in the mists and shadows of prehistoric human life. All we know is that we find traces of what we think of as religious consciousness and practices in the historical remains of the earliest human communities. So, as far as we can see, it does not appear that religion is something humans invented partway through their known historical experience on earth, as we did irrigation and automobiles. This confirms the suspicion, implied in the preceding section, that religion is somehow very basic to, perhaps constitutive of, the life of human animals.

14. Christian Smith, "Secularizing American Higher Education: The Case of Early American Sociology," in Smith, *The Secular Revolution*.

Having despaired of locating the historical origins of human religion, many other scholars have instead explored the social, functional, or psychological origins of religion. The French sociologist Emile Durkheim and the Austrian psychologist Sigmund Freud are famous among the classical writers.[15] And after some decades of an apparent lack of scholarly interest in religious origins—indeed, of a complete theoretical stagnation in the field—recent years have seen a surge in new books purporting to explain the ultimate source of religion, two of which I take the time to mention here.[16] Fordham University anthropologist Stewart Guthrie, for one, argues in his 1993 book *Faces in the Clouds: A New Theory of Religion* that religion is the result of an anthropomorphizing strategy that is rational (even if deceiving) in an uncertain, ambiguous world in need of interpretation:

> We animate and anthropomorphize because, when we see something as alive or humanlike, we can take precautions. If we see it as alive we can, for example, stalk it or flee. If we see it as humanlike, we can try to establish a social relationship. If it turns out not to be alive or humanlike, we usually lose little by having thought it was. This practice yields more in occasional big successes than it costs in frequent little failures. In short, animism and anthropomorphizing stem from the principle, "better safe than sorry."[17]

Guthrie's theory, in other words, is an evolutionary version of rational choice theory that emphasizes the limits of human perceptions and hu-

15. Emile Durkheim, *The Elementary Forms of Religious Life* (New York: Free Press, 1915); Sigmund Freud, *The Origins of Religion* (New York: Harmondsworth Penguin, 1985).

16. Others include Pascal Boyer, *The Naturalness of Religious Ideas* (Berkeley: University of California Press, 1994); Pascal Boyer, *Religion Explained: The Evolutionary Origins of Religious Thought* (New York: Basic Books, 2001); John Schumaker, *The Corruption of Reality: A Unified Theory of Religion, Hypnosis, and Psychopathology* (Amherst, Mass.: Prometheus, 1995); Michael Winkelman, *Shamanism: The Neural Ecology of Consciousness and Healing* (Westport, Conn.: Bergin and Garvey, 2000); Eugene d'Aquili and Andrew Newberg, "The Neuropsychological Basis of Religion, or Why God Won't Go Away," *Zygon: Journal of Religion and Science* 33 (1995): 187–201.

17. Stewart Guthrie, *Faces in the Clouds: A New Theory of Religion* (New York: Oxford University Press, 1993), 5.

man tendencies toward risk aversion, which together caused early humans to "attribute humanity to the world" by making god in the human image.

Another recent work reviving the quest for the origins of religion is Elizabeth City State University sociologist James McClenon's 2002 book *Wondrous Healing: Shamanism, Human Evolution, and the Origin of Religion*. McClenon advances a theory that he claims is based on evolutionary neurophysiology, is subject to empirical evaluation, and integrates the most important aspects of all previous theories. He argues, in short, that human religious belief has evolved from the success of ancient healing rituals that employed hypnotic suggestion to reduce stress and suffering, which eventually generated therapeutic shamanistic rituals involving verbal suggestion. Since early humans practiced these ritual healings for a period of time sufficiently long that "genes associated with hypnotizability" were "selected for" through processes of natural selection, their human decedents (us) have inherited a "biological propensity for religious belief and ritual." For this reason, McClenon says, human religious propensities have an ultimately biological basis and have been formed in us through evolutionary processes.[18]

The back cover of McClenon's book claims that it is "controversial and daring." The back cover of Guthrie's declares that his "explanation is radical" and that he "argues persuasively." I myself find neither of them to be any of those things. They are not controversial, daring, radical, or persuasive. If readers today so happen to find them plausible and important, it is not because they have resolved any of the empirical or intellectual problems that beset the many similar theories that preceded them. Nor is it because they advance any great theoretical breakthrough or insight.[19] Rather, it is because they conform so well to the two major theoretical traditions in ascendancy in academia today: neo-Darwinian evolutionism and rational choice theory. Indeed, these books are remarkably conventional in their implicit and explicit reliance on the assumptions of natural selection, functionalism, rational egoism, and atheism.

18. James McClenon, *Wondrous Healing: Shamanism, Human Evolution, and the Origin of Religion* (Dekalb: Northern Illinois University Press, 2002). Quotes are on pp. 4, 45.

19. On Paul Boyer's *Religion Explained*, see Paul Griffiths, "Faith Seeking Explanation," *First Things* 119 (January 2002): 53–57.

Here, by contrast, is a theory that would be truly controversial, daring, and radical: human religions have existed and do exist everywhere because a God really does actually exist, and many humans—especially those not blinded by the reigning narratives of modern science and academia—feel a recurrent and deeply compelling "built-in" desire to know and worship, in their various ways, the God who is there. Try publishing that, and we will find out who is controversial and daring. Of course, that theory, while not empirically verifiable, would certainly explain a lot. It is a most parsimonious theory. But prevailing assumptions of knowledge production rule it inadmissible. So we stick with other theories no more empirically verifiable or intellectually coherent but that at least fit our dominant narrative.

The sociology of religion is a field currently divided between two disputed paradigms,[20] neither of which, it turns out, has much helpful to say about religious origins. The theoretical tradition that has come by default to be labeled the "old paradigm" is perhaps best represented by Peter Berger's book *The Sacred Canopy: Elements of a Sociological Theory of Religion.*[21] In all fairness, Berger never explicitly claims to be trying to explain the origins of religion per se—although the first third of his argument very much reflects this interest. In it, Berger conveys what very many people, myself included, take to be an eloquent and insightful sociological account of the basis of human culture, habit, organization, socialization, and ideological legitimations. But what is strange for a book about religion is how abruptly and without explication religion simply plops into the book. Having set a very interesting theoretical stage with its discussion of world-openness, meaning, chaos, order, externalization, objectivation, internalization, legitimation, and so on, "religion" suddenly shows up on page 25 with the simple declaration: "Religion is the human enterprise by which a sacred cosmos is established." Being quite familiar with the existence of religion, we readers accept its introduction thus and read on.

20. Steven Warner, "Works in Progress toward a New Paradigm for the Sociology of Religion in the United States," *American Journal of Sociology* 98, no. 5 (1993): 1044–93.

21. Peter Berger, *The Sacred Canopy: Elements of a Sociological Theory of Religion* (Garden City, N.J.: Anchor Books, 1968).

But I suggest that we would do well to go back and consider this question: why does the world that Berger elaborates in pages 1–24 ever need or invent the religion that drops in on page 25? Why is there any necessity for this thing "religion"? What is clear in Berger's account is why the world he describes needs and creates order in the form of humanly constructed culture. But, given all of Berger's premises and arguments, there is no apparent reason why that order would need to have anything other than immanent sources, referents, and legitimations. Why could not humans in the course of their evolutionary history simply construct "reality" as a bulwark against the terrors of chaos—without reference to anything sacred—and pass on that immanently, empirically grounded "reality" to their children with different versions of the legitimating explanation "This is simply the way things are"; and then socially control through punishment those few who do not conform? Why in Berger's theoretical system should religion have ever arisen among socially constructing humans in the first place?

The closest Berger ever gets to answering this question is indirectly through his brief observation that religions provide a certain ultimacy to ideological legitimations. It is somehow more convincing, apparently, to say that our reality has been ordained by the gods than to say that our reality is simply the way thing are. But that only raises the questions of why or how in a world actually without gods the idea of "the gods" would have ever popped into anyone's head; and why such an empirically groundless idea would enjoy such widespread credibility so as to be able to provide the ultimate legitimation of reality itself. Such an account suggests that religion was perhaps the invention of the powerful to defend their own status and privilege; or perhaps of the powerless to explain to themselves and make sufferable their own deprivation (Marx lurks just below the surface here). But my questions remain. Why in a spiritless and godless world would people ever conceive of spirits and gods in the first place? And why ever embrace nonempirical constructions that function to exclude one from the empirical goods of the powerful and privileged? It is hard to believe, if the need for ultimacy in legitimation was religion's actual origin, that religion would have continued to be as strong and widespread as it has in the modern world (unless, perhaps, this is where the "selected upon" genetic propensity toward religious belief comes in, which changes the discussion entirely). Durkheim (the atheist) was not wrong in arguing that something as powerful as religion could not be based finally on an error.[22]

But that is not all, for this reading of Berger's account of religious origins faces yet another theoretical difficulty. It is a well-known fallacy of functionalist theories to argue that because something serves a particular function that that functionality itself explains why the thing exists. My wife serves the function of keeping me somewhat humble, but that is not why she became and is my wife, why our marriage exists. And the mere fact that religions may have at times and places legitimated the privileges of the powerful—which, not incidentally, it does not always do[23]—does not itself necessarily explain religion's existence. It only leaves us in speculation. To be clear, none of this is necessarily a critique of Berger per se, since, as I said, he does not claim to explain the origins of religion. It is merely an observation that *The Sacred Canopy* actually offers no convincing account for why humans are so chronically and pervasively religious. One suspects that, as he was operating out of the Lutheran tradition, Berger's own thinking on this point may have finally resorted more to a theological than radically constructionist framework.

Up against what is now labeled the old paradigm has arisen a contentious "new paradigm" in the sociology of religion, represented in part by Rodney Stark and Roger Finke's book *Acts of Faith: Explaining the Human*

22. "It is an essential postulate of sociology that a human institution cannot rest upon an error and a lie, without which it could not exist. If it were not founded in the nature of things, it would have encountered in the facts a resistance over which it could never have triumphed. . . . In reality, then, there are no religions which are false." Durkheim, *Elementary Forms of Religious Life*, 14–15.

23. See, for example, Christian Smith (ed.), *Disruptive Religion: The Force of Faith in Social Movement Activism* (New York: Routledge, 1996); Christian Smith, *The Emergence of Liberation Theology: Radical Religion and Social Movement Theory* (Chicago: University of Chicago Press, 1991); Christian Smith, *Resisting Reagan: The U.S. Central America Peace Movement* (Chicago: University of Chicago Press, 1996); Charles Marsh, *God's Long Summer: Stories of Faith and Civil Rights* (Princeton, N.J.: Princeton University Press, 1997); Matthew Moen and Lowell Gustafson (eds.), *The Religious Challenge to the State* (Philadelphia: Temple University Press, 1992).

Side of Religion.[24] The book—as I myself say in a blurb on its back cover—has very many fine merits, in my view, as does the new paradigm as a whole. But explaining the origins of religion is not one of them. In fact, I think Stark and Finke fail badly at it, and it is worth considering how and why. (Since I understand that Stark is the lead author of the chapter in question, I will hereafter refer to him alone as its author.)

Stark's theory of religious origins is explicitly grounded on the assumptions of rational choice theory: "Within the limits of their information and understanding, restricted by available options, guided by their preferences and tastes, humans attempt to make rational choices. . . . It makes sense to model religion as the behavior of rational, reasonably well informed actors who choose to 'consume' religious 'commodities' in the same way that they weigh the costs and benefits of consuming secular commodities." In the old days, when religion was readily dismissed as irrational fantasy, it was easy to explain the origins of religion as arising from the fear and ignorance of savages. Stark handily dispenses with such nonsense, however, and asserts instead that religion is no less rational than any other human activity. So far so good. But that leaves Stark with a new difficulty to explain: why rationally self-interested calculators of costs and benefits would freely choose to sacrifice for and invest in non-empirical beings offering only unverifiable and chronologically distant rewards. Given all of the options, is that a rationally self-interested move to make? Stark's answer is yes, because certain rewards for which humans have high demands are unverifiable and available only in the distant future. Religion, in other words, really is just another source of rewards and benefits that people seek to maximize or "satisfice" through social exchanges. The only difference is that religion offers *a particular kind* of demanded reward, and to get it one must exchange not with humans but the gods. Otherwise, religion is like any other product, activity, service, or commodity: it exists in a market to satisfy human preferences and desires. Let us call this the Starkian world.

But what then is the actual source of human religion? Where does it

24. Rodney Stark and Roger Finke, *Acts of Faith: Explaining the Human Side of Religion* (Berkeley: University of California Press, 2000). The following quotes are from pp. 38, 42–43. On the unverifiability and future distance of religious rewards, see p. 88. The "evil gods" quote comes from p. 98.

come from? Why do people conceive and demand it? Like Berger, ironically, Stark never explains. Just as with the archetypal work of the old
paradigm, religion simply plops theoretically into Stark's theory, on pages
88–91: "Otherworldly rewards are those that will be obtained only in a
nonempirical (usually posthumous) context. . . . Supernatural refers to
forces or entities beyond or outside nature that can suspend, alter, or
ignore physical forces. . . . Gods are supernatural 'beings' having consciousness and desire. . . . Religion consists of very general explanations of
existence, including the terms of exchange with a god or gods." There is
nowhere in this discussion any explication of where religion or gods or
supernatural *came from*, no explanation for how they ever got into the
Starkian world in the first place. Particularly baffling is how and why "evil
gods"—which "intend to inflict coercive exchanges or deceptions on humans, resulting from losses for human exchange partners"—ever make
their way into the Starkian world. Would rationally self-interested people
invent costly evil gods if they did not actually exist?

Whether or not Stark's theory works if one presumes that people *are*
religious or that gods actually *do* exist, it certainly does not work as an
account explaining *why* people are religious. Even more than in Berger's
meaning-and-order-oriented theoretical world, there is no apparent reason why in a Starkian exchange-and-reward-oriented world, given its rational choice assumptions, humans would generate and sustain this thing
we call religion. Consider the following problems. The feasibility of Stark's
theory depends on rational people concocting the existence of spiritual
beings that are, in a presumably materialist world, in no way a part of
their actual reality. Why would rational people do such a thing? Because,
Stark says, they have a demand for particular rewards that only such
nonexisting spiritual beings can supply. But why would rational people
ever conceive of and continue to demand a reward that actually does not
exist and that they in fact cannot and will not enjoy? I, for example,
imagine that I would find it immensely rewarding to go to the next Olympics and win five gold medals, but that is in fact an impossibility; and to
the extent that I am a *rational* person I realize this and construct my
reward expectation structure in a way that does not even consider the
possibility of competing successfully in the Olympics. To be able to win
the five medals would be a tremendous gain. But the fact that I cannot
is not a terrible loss. It simply is. Likewise, people in a purely materialist

world might find the idea—if indeed they could first conceive it—of eternal life in heaven, for example, very attractive. But if they are rational materialists they would realize that such a thing is an impossibility and will revise their reward expectations accordingly (as many people that I know who do believe that we live in a materialist world have done). They will focus instead on chocolate and skiing and sex and careers, which actually can be rewarding. To persist in sacrificing for and investing in an impossibility would be quite irrational—at which point the Starkian world begins to melt down. Perhaps the reward rational people seek in religion is not heaven itself, but only the comfort of imagining and anticipating heaven? Perhaps. But that solution also cuts the legs out from under Starkian rationality, resuscitating the view of religion as an escapist illusion of foolish daydreamers that Stark had so nicely dispensed with. In order to hold onto rationality at one level (self-interested reward maximization), Stark must either posit irrationality at another level (invention of [nonexistent] good and evil gods) or concede explicitly that the gods really do exist (which, given our dominant academic narrative, is itself a form of irrationality).

If the new rational choice paradigm in religion has an essential, perhaps fatal problem—an intellectual "original sin," so to speak—it is not its premise that religious actors are rational. It is rather its premise that religion is essentially and ultimately about acquisition and satisfaction through exchange. Once this assumption is posited, a number of problems ensue, only one of which is rational choice's inability to explain the origins of religion, despite its sustained attempts to do so. This is because humans are not at bottom calculating, consuming animals. They are moral, believing animals. And rational choice theory is incapable of making adequate sense of moral, believing animals. A different approach is needed.

How else, then, might we understand religious origins? What account could make sense of the fact that so many people in the world have been and are religious? Let us begin by considering the theistic theory mentioned earlier: human religions have existed and do exist pervasively because a God really does exist, and most humans feel a recurrent and deeply compelling desire to know and worship, in their various ways, the God who is there. How does this explanation fare? First, the theistic assumption in this theory is not empirically verifiable. But then again, neither are the evolutionarily "selected-upon" religion genes that allegedly generate human propensities toward religious belief and practice that today purport to explain religion scientifically. More broadly, this old model of theoretical science as proceeding solely on empirical verification and falsification is philosophically defective and theoretically outmoded.[25] Second, since not all scholars are theists, the proposed theistic theory violates the precept that scientific inquiry and knowledge should be universal and neutral—accessible to any scholar whatever his or her own personal belief commitments. But then again, the alternative theoretical explanations proposed by sociobiology, evolutionary psychology, exchange theory, and rational choice currently in ascendancy in the academy are also neither neutral nor universal but similarly require commitment to sets of particular ontological assumptions and beliefs in order to be remotely plausible. And many scholars, this author included, cannot and do not accept those assumptions and beliefs. More broadly, we know that no science operates as a universal and neutral enterprise, that all science necessarily relies on particular presuppositions, paradigms, and research programs

25 In brief, Sir Karl Popper, among others, successfully criticized the tradition running at least from Francis Bacon to logical positivism claiming that scientific truth requires verification through inductive generalization, by arguing (a) that infallible foundations of knowledge are not accessible, since human capacities of perception and intellect are restricted to bounded comprehensions of our world; (b) that since verification of a universal theory requires a positive finding in every case, most of which remain forever in the inaccessible future, verification can therefore never be achieved with certitude; and (c) that the verification standard itself could not be verified, so it does not qualify as meaningful according to its own requirement. See Karl Popper, *The Logic of Scientific Discovery* (New York: Basic Books, 1959 [1934]). Yet Popper's own theory of "falsificationism"—that is, of reliance on deductive falsification to identify "correct" theories as those which have not yet been proven wrong—was subsequently largely discredited, since (a) it provides no logical grounds for preferring one theory over another, as an as yet unfalsified theory is just as capable of being actually wrong than its recently falsified forerunner; and since (b) falsificationism does not represent the actual history of scientific discovery, in which theory and data often do not easily correspond and in which some very good theories have appeared originally to have been falsified. See George Couvalis, *The Philosophy of Science* (Thousand Oaks, Calif.: Sage Publications, 1997); Imre Lakatos and Alan Musgrave (eds.), *Criticism and the Growth of Knowledge* (Cambridge: Cambridge University Press, 1970).

that are believed in and committed to by specific scholarly communities of practice.[26] Third, the theistic theory proposed earlier will violate the cultural sensibilities of many modern academics and so create controversy and division.[27] Perhaps. But so what? Sociobiology, evolutionary psychology, exchange theory, and rational choice violate the cultural sensibilities

26. Thomas Kuhn, *The Structure of Scientific Revolutions* (Chicago: University of Chicago Press, 1962); Paul Feyerabend, *Against Method* (London: Verso, 1975); Imre Lakatos, *The Methodology of Scientific Research Programmes: Philosophical Papers, Volume 1*, ed. John Worrall and Gregory Currie (Cambridge: Cambridge University Press, 1978); Helen Longino, *Science as Social Knowledge* (Princeton, N.J.: Princeton University Press, 1990); Steven Shapin, *A Social History of Truth* (Chicago: University of Chicago Press, 1994); Steven Shapin, *The Scientific Revolution* (Chicago: University of Chicago Press, 1996); Robert Proctor, *Value-Free Science?* (Cambridge: Harvard University Press, 1991); Sergio Sismondo, *Science without Myth: On Construction, Reality, and Social Knowledge* (Albany: State University of New York Press, 1996); Michael Polanyi, *Science, Faith, and Society* (Chicago: University of Chicago Press, 1946); Michael Polanyi, *Personal Knowledge: Toward a Post-Critical Philosophy* (Chicago: University of Chicago Press, 1958); Michael Polanyi, *The Tacit Dimension* (New York: Doubleday, 1966).

27. Aside from other concerns, some may think that theism is known philosophically to be irrational or nonsensical, yet that is now a philosophically discredited view; see, for example, William Alston, "Knowledge of God," in Marcus Hester (ed.), *Faith, Reason, and Skepticism* (Philadelphia: Temple University Press, 1992); William Alston, *Perceiving God* (Ithaca, N.Y.: Cornell University Press, 1991); Alvin Plantinga, *Warranted Christian Belief* (Oxford: Oxford University Press, 2000); Alvin Plantinga, *Warrant and Proper Function* (Oxford: Oxford University Press, 1993); Alvin Plantinga, *Warrant: The Current Debate* (Oxford: Oxford University Press, 1993); Alvin Plantinga and Nicholas Wolterstorff (eds.), *Faith and Rationality* (Notre Dame, Ind.: University of Notre Dame Press, 1983); Nicholas Wolterstorff, *Reason within the Bounds of Religion* (Grand Rapids, Mich.: Eerdmans, 1976). Even Richard Rorty has conceded this change in views of theism: "Plantinga's *God and Other Minds* is quite convincing on many points, and I admire Wolterstorff's *Reason within the Bounds of Religion*. . . . I admire them both as remarkable philosophers . . . [who] show why we atheists should stop praising ourselves for being more 'rational' than theists. On this point they seem to me quite right" (quoted in Stephen Louthan, "On Religion—A Discussion with Richard Rorty, Alvin Plantinga and Nicholas Wolterstorff," *Christian Scholar's Review* 27, no. 2 [1996]: 179).

of many academics, this author included, yet that does not preclude their serious consideration as theoretical explanations. Moreover, concern about the creation of controversy and division is simply an irrelevant factor in determining the merits of a theoretical explanation. Or do we think that Galileo should have buried his proposed astronomical system in order to avoid controversy and division?

It is true that a theistic theory of religious origins is ruled inadmissible by the currently dominant narrative of science and is profoundly out of step with the last, say, 120 years of related American scholarship.[28] But the reasons for that at this stage of our understanding of science and human knowing seem to have much more to do with cultural, political, and perhaps emotional disapproval of the idea than actual and compelling intellectual objections to it. And so I am inclined to leave the matter here and maintain the parsimonious theistic explanation as my proposed theory.[29]

28. See Robert Shepard, *God's People in the Ivory Tower* (Brooklyn: Carlson Publishing, 1991). In historical terms this is a novel situation, however, since, for most of human history there simply would have been no need to explain religious origins nontheistically. Only in a modern, secular, Enlightenment context would explaining religious origins nontheistically be a meaningful and pressing problem. See J. Samuel Preus, *Explaining Religion: Criticism and Theory from Bodin to Freud* (New Haven, Conn.: Yale University Press, 1987); Frank Manuel, *The Eighteenth Century Confronts the Gods* (Cambridge: Harvard University Press, 1959); Frank Manuel, *The Changing of the Gods* (Hanover, N.H.: Brown University Press, 1983). But for centuries in the West before that, the question of the wellspring of religious faith, including diversities of religious faiths, would have been most often answered in theistic terms. See, for example, Samuel Purchas, *Purchas His Pilgrimage; or, Relations of the World and the Religions Observed in All Ages and Places Discovered, In Foure Parts* (London: Printed by William Stansby for Henrie Fetherstone, 1613); Matthew Tindal, *Christianity as Old as the Creation; or, The Gospel, a Republication of the Religion of Nature* (London, 1730).

29. Stated in somewhat different, if philosophically disputable, terms, this approach suggests that the objects of human desires are normally existent, and that human desires derive at least in part from their need for or serious interest in the objects of their desires. For example, the object of hunger is food, and people feel hungry because food exists and people need it to live; the object of erotic desire is sex, and people feel this desire because sex exists and people both need it to

For the sake of a more inclusive discussion, however, I will attempt here to articulate a not-incompatible theory of religious origins perhaps more accessible to a broader audience. What follows hinges not only on the model of moral, believing animals developed earlier, but also (as did the account of human morality in chapter 2) on the centrality of the problem of human transcendent self-consciousness in a finite, non-self-interpreting world, perhaps best expressed in Reinhold Niebuhr's 1938–40 Gifford Lectures. Niebuhr was the leading American liberal Protestant theologian of the mid–twentieth century, yet his thinking on this point fundamentally followed that of the 1901–2 Gifford Lectures by the non-theist William James.[30]

First, moral, believing, narrating animals—as opposed to both rational, acquisitive, exchanging animals and genetically adaptive and governed animals—are the kind of creatures about whom it is not odd to think that they would develop beliefs, symbols, and practices about the reality of a superempirical order that makes claims to organize and guide human life. As moral animals, humans are inescapably interested in and guided by normative cultural orders that specify what is good, right, true, beautiful, worthy, noble, and just in life, and what is not. To be a human person, to possess an identity, to act with agency requires locating one's life within a larger moral order by which to know who one is and how one ought to live. Human individuals and groups, therefore, must look beyond themselves for sources of moral order that are understood as not established by their own desires, decisions, or preferences but instead believed to exist apart from them, providing standards by which their desires, decisions, and preferences can themselves be judged. As believing animals, human faith in superempirical

---

procreate and want it for pleasure. This suggests—and to be clear, only suggests—the possibility that the persistent, recurrent, and widespread human desire to know about, communicate with, and worship or make sacrifices to gods or a God suggests that an object of that desire exists—which, perhaps through the "implantation" or otherwise building-in of that desire—itself generates the felt human desire in question. See Robert Holyer, "The Argument from Desire," *Faith and Philosophy* 5, no. 1 (1988): 61–71.

30. As shown by the 2001 Gifford Lectures of Stanley Hauerwas, published in *With the Grain of the Universe* (Grand Rapids, Mich.: Brazos Press, 2001).

orders that make claims to organize and guide human life is not cate-gorically different from the fundamental and continual acts of presup-posing and believing in all of the other assumptions and ideas that make the living of life even possible. The standard distinction between faith and fact is a false dichotomy. What we take as facts are always de-pendent on and meaningful in terms of worldviews that ultimately rest on empirically unverifiable belief commitments and suppositions. So humans being religious—that is, believing in and living their lives with reference to the superempirical orders that define religion—is episte-mologically more in continuity with the living of ordinary human life as a whole than not. It is typically believers in certain modern, Enlight-enment narratives that construct reality in ways that obfuscate the faith-based character of human existence who insist on the (erroneous) faith/fact distinction. Finally, as narrating animals who experience life as lived through time and who seek to make meaning of life and self through life-constituting and orienting narratives of many sorts, the superempir-ical orders of religion provide humans with compelling narratives link-ing cosmic, historical, and personal significance for individuals and communities across time. Humans most typically know about their su-perempirical orders through religious traditions passed on through time in narrative form. The enlightenment of Buddha; the revelation to Mo-hamed; the Exodus from Egypt and ascent to Mount Sinai; the death and resurrection of Jesus of Nazareth; the works of Brahma, Vishnu, and Shiva; the creation and ordering of the world by the Shinto Kami, Izanagi-no-mikoto and Izanami-no-mikoto, and so on are narrative em-plotments of truth and worth that derive from superempirical orders. In sum, the human condition and the character of religion quite naturally fit, cohere, complement, and reinforce each other.

Yet this anthropologically referenced account still only so far suggests that it is plausible that the kind of animals I have described humans to be could very well be religious in the terms I have described religion to be. I have, however, not yet suggested why humans would or should work out their moral, believing, narrating character in specifically religious terms. Do we have good reason to think that religion would "show up" in the world that I have in this book described? Again, provisionally set-ting aside a theistic account answering this question, how might we ex-plain the specific need or interest or desire of moral, believing animals to inhabit orders that are not only moral but also superempirical in their sources of the moral?

The short answer to that question, I suggest, is that self, life, history, and the world are not self-interpreting in meaning. In order to make sense of the meaning of self, life, history, and the world, one *has to* get outside of them, to "transcend" them, and interpret them within horizons and frameworks of perspective derived from beyond the object of interpretation.[31] I have already argued the point with regard to the human self. Individual humans are not self-generating, self-defining, self-understanding creatures. Individual humans only, always, and can ever enjoy life, identity, and significance by locating themselves within stories and cultural orders outside and beyond themselves, in terms of which their lives have place and purpose. This is an elementary sociological insight. But the same is true for life, history, and the world. They are not self-interpreting. They need a transcendent horizon or framework of understanding derived from above and beyond themselves to be given significance.

Again, in this I am directly following Reinhold Niebuhr, who emphasizes the tension inherent in the paradoxical human experience of simultaneous finitude as material animals and transcendence in self-consciousness:

> The human spirit has the special capacity of standing continuously outside itself in terms of indefinite regression. Consciousness is a capacity for surveying the world and determining action from a governing center. Self-consciousness represents a further degree of transcendence in which the self makes itself its own object in such a way that the ego is finally always subject and not object. . . . The self knows the world, insofar as it knows the world, because it stands outside both itself and the world, which means that it cannot understand itself except as it is understood from beyond itself and the world.[32]

31. For an informing discussion of the concepts of horizons and frameworks, see Charles Taylor, *Sources of the Self* (Cambridge: Harvard University Press, 1989), 16–52.

32. Reinhold Niebuhr, *The Nature and Destiny of Man, Vol. 1* (New York: Charles Scribner's Sons, 1964 [1948]), 13–14. The following quotes come from pp. 164–65, 141, 14.

The transcendence inherent in this human self-consciousness creates conditions that for meaning require interpretive frameworks or perspectives that transcend the object of interpretation and the interpreter him or herself:

> Implicit in the human situation of freedom and in man's capacity to transcend himself and his world is his inability to construct a world of meaning without finding a source and key to the structure of meaning which transcends the world beyond his own capacity to transcend it. . . . The problem is not solved without the introduction of a principle of meaning which transcends the world of meaning to be interpreted. . . . If the effort is made to comprehend the meaning of the world through the principle of natural causation alone, the world is conceived in terms of a mechanistic coherence which has no place for the freedom which reveals itself in human consciousness. . . . Furthermore a mind which transcends itself cannot legitimately make itself the ultimate principle of interpretation by which it explains the relation of mind to the world.

In this way, history itself can have no meaning except through interpretative understandings that come not from within but beyond history, which are always acquired through believed-in presuppositions of one kind or another:

> It is . . . impossible to interpret history at all without a principle of interpretation which history as such does not yield. The various principles of interpretation current in modern culture . . . are all principles of historical interpretation introduced by faith. They claim to be conclusions about the nature of history at which men arrive after a "scientific" analysis of the course of events; but there can be no such analysis of the course of events which does not make use of some presuppositions of faith, as the principle of analysis and interpretation.

The life of the individual human self, too, needs a framework of interpretation or understanding that comes from beyond, yet is related to and through, empirical history:

> The meaning of life transcends the meaning of history. . . . History, however meaningful, cannot give life its full meaning. Each individual transcends and is involved in the historical process. Insofar as he is involved in history,

the disclosure of life's meaning must come to him in history. Insofar as he transcends history, the source of life's meaning must transcend history.[33]

This situation inherent in the tension and paradox of finite yet self-conscious humanity thus leads humans naturally, according to Niebuhr, toward nonempirical orders of religion as transcendent interpretive principles of significance for humans searching to understand the meaning of themselves, life, history, the world, and the cosmos: "The fact of self-transcendence leads inevitably to the search for a God who transcends the world."[34] Thus, Niebuhr claims, "history cannot find its meaning except in the disclosure of a divine sovereignty, which both governs and transcends it."[35] For these reasons "this essential homelessness of the human spirit is the ground of all religion; for the self which stands outside itself and the world cannot find the meaning of life in itself or the world."

This account of religious origins—though constructed from an anthropological and not a theological point of view—is entirely compatible and complementary with the theistic account of religious origins offered above. At the same time, it does not necessarily depend on that theistic account for plausibility. If Hauerwas is right, as I believe he is, the atheist William James would have been entirely satisfied with my interpretation of Niebuhr's theory for an account of religious origins.[36]

Finally, all of this re-raises the more basic question of how and why humans in fact are not only finite, material animals but also self-conscious, transcendent animals. Here I simply repeat the same answer I gave in chapter 2. Perhaps it is because of the relatively large brains our species have acquired through long evolutionary development, which are neurologically capable of depths and complexities of self-consciousness unavailable to smaller brained animals. Or perhaps it is because humans are uniquely created "in the image" of a personal, conscious, self-

33. Reinhold Niebuhr, *The Nature and Destiny of Man*, Vol. 2 (New York: Charles Scribner's Sons, 1964 [1948]), 36.

34. Niebuhr, *The Nature and Destiny of Man*, Vol. 1, 165. The "homelessness" quote below comes from p. 14.

35. Niebuhr, *The Nature and Destiny of Man*, Vol. 2, 36.

36. Hauerwas, *With the Grain of the Universe*. A more fully developed account, however, would have to explore historical variations in the inwardness of self-consciousness, suggested, for example, by Taylor, *Sources of the Self*.

conscious, and transcendent God. Or perhaps it is both. The reader's own metanarrative and most deeply embraced moral order will provide the answer for him or her. I likewise myself know what I believe to be true.

Conclusion

This chapter has not tried to say everything that might be said about religion. Its goal has been rather more modest. I have tried to offer a sociologically useful definition of religion. I have attempted to explain how that definition may help us better understand religious persistence and secularization, religious influences in life and the lack thereof, and the character of belief and "unbelief." I have sought to engage the theoretical question of religious origins, arguing in particular that neither sociobiological nor rational choice theories of religious origins can succeed in persuasively accounting for the sources, persistence, and prevalence of religion. Instead, I have proposed an account of religious origins based on the human experience of self-consciousness and transcendence giving rise to the need for interpretations of meaning that have sources above and beyond that which is interpreted. I have suggested that this account is at once entirely congenial with, yet not necessarily dependent on, a theistic account of religious origins. In all of this I have attempted to work out of the framework of the moral, believing account of the human animal developed in earlier chapters.

THE RETURN OF CULTURE?

American sociology has in recent years witnessed a revived interest in culture and cultural analysis. For some time now we have been hearing about a major "cultural turn" in the academy, a "spectacular resurgence of interest in culture" that has spawned a "frenetic rush to the study of culture." We are told that "a kind of academic culture mania has set in" and that "the sociology of culture has been virtually reinvented."[1] Culture, it seems, has made a big comeback in sociology.

This return of culture in sociology represents something of an intellectual pendulum swing. Talcott Parsons's structural functionalism dominated the middle decades of the twentieth century. It taught that human societies are regulated and coordinated from the top down by their cultural systems and that, from the bottom up, individual actors are oriented

1. For the sources of these quotes, see Victoria Bonnell and Lynn Hunt, *Beyond the Cultural Turn* (Berkeley: University of California Press, 1999), 5; Ewa Morawska and Willfried Spohn, " 'Cultural Pluralism' in Historical Sociology," in Diana Crane (ed.), *The Sociology of Culture*, 45–90 (Cambridge: Blackwell, 1994), 45; William H. Sewell Jr., "The Concept(s) of Culture," in Bonnell and Hunt, *Beyond the Cultural Turn*, 36, 37; and Diana Crane, "Introduction: The Challenge of the Sociology of Culture to Sociology as a Discipline," in Crane, *The Sociology of Culture*, 1.

and guided by cultural values that they internalize through socialization. In the mid-1960s and 1970s, however, Parsons's structural functionalism was attacked and displaced as the dominant framework in the discipline. Its critics charged, among other things, that the actors it described were mere "cultural dopes" and that the cultural value system that it said integrated society left little room for social difference, conflict, and change. None of that seemed to comport with the social reality of "the Sixties." An assortment of new theoretical schools and frameworks then vied to replace the old functionalist system: conflict theory, neo-Marxisms, rational choice theory, "structuralist" analysis, symbolic interactionism and ethnomethodology, network analysis, and more. Most of these had little interest in concepts like values, norms, beliefs, and social roles associated with the marginalized Parsonian theory. Culture was out. Structure, conflict, and rationality—all thought to be *not* culture—were in.

But by the 1980s it was becoming increasingly clear that many of the theoretical schools and approaches that had displaced structural functionalism were running up against problems and limitations built into their own systems. Many of these related to the difficulty of providing compelling social explanations without reference to something like a larger normative order that earlier scholars would have called culture.[2] Neo-Marxists confronted the difficulties of viewing the entire "superstructure" as a mere reflection of the means and relations of economic production and struggled to find new ways to account for human agency and the "semi-autonomy" of culture. Many sociologists came to realize that conflict theory had simply inverted structural functionalism's emphasis on order and equilibrium and thus merely reproduced its one-sidedness instead of offering greater theoretical complexity and sophistication. Symbolic interactionism, while focusing on the intentions of interacting subjects, seemed unable to account for the profound influence on interaction of the larger normative and institutional contexts within which interaction takes place. Rational choice theory, which promised rigorous analytical explanation and prediction based on a few simple assumptions, began to run afoul of its key premise that self-interested actors who hold stable

2. Jeffrey Alexander, *Action and Its Environments* (New York: Columbia University Press, 1988), esp. 11–45.

preferences seek to maximize material benefits and rewards. It turned out that preferences are not particularly stable, interests do not always appear to be selfish, and valued goods are often not material. Developments in structure, conflict, rationality, and interaction in the 1970s clearly expanded our sociological vision. But the theoretical approaches that had overthrown the Parsonian system seemed to have left out something important in social life.

In response, a number of scholars began to call for a reclamation of culture in sociological analysis. Various developments within and outside of sociology—in semiotics, social constructionism, poststructuralism, studies of symbolic production, interpretive anthropology, ritual studies, narrative analysis, and more—had helped prepare the intellectual ground for new and creative sociological scholarship that began to employ culture in ways more sophisticated than structural functionalism had. Some of the scholars who were important in producing this renovation of cultural analysis in sociology were Jeffrey Alexander, Robert Wuthnow, Ann Swidler, William Sewell Jr., Margaret Somers, Wendy Griswold, Craig Calhoun, Michael Shudson, Michèle Lamont, and others. These in turn had often drawn variously on and modified the works of Pierre Bourdieu, Mary Douglas, Clifford Geertz, Michel Foucault, Marshall Sahlins, Daniel Bell, Raymond Williams, E. P. Thompson, Robert Bellah, Stuart Hall, Jürgen Habermas, and other seminal social theorists. Increasingly, in the late 1980s, American sociologists were talking in their analyses about cultural structures, communities of discourse, cultural toolkits, symbolic representation, cultural capital, discursive formations, cultural practices, and the like. The advance over the old functionalist treatment of culture was great, and the fruits of this new cultural sociology have been many. As a result, we enjoy rich and varied insights into cultural production and reception, symbols and cognition, discursive categories and historical change, language and power, and more.

But for all of the value and insight in the new cultural sociology, something important, I would like to suggest, is still missing. Something that was lost in the rejection of structural functionalism—however inadequate that framework was—remains lost, not only in the many un-cultural theoretical approaches that followed in functionalism's wake but also in much of recent sociological work in culture. What is missing, and problematically so, I suggest, is *a convincing account of human motivation,* one that is empirically credible and theoretically sound.[3] Below I address more fully why human motivation matters, but first I need to establish the point of its absence. The lack of convincing accounts of human motivation in cultural theory is evident in the literature in two distinct ways. In some works of cultural sociology, the question of human motivation is simply left unaddressed. Other works do proceed with more explicit assumptions about human motivation, but they are often assumptions, I will argue, that undermine the project of cultural analysis itself by reducing culture to an instrumental means to achieve allegedly non–culturally determined ends.

In the following pages I attempt to explain my suggestion that much of contemporary cultural sociology lacks a convincing account of human motivation, and why this is a problem. I will not go into tremendous depth in elaborating this critique. It will suffice instead to examine briefly a sample of cultural theorists from the 1980s and 1990s—Pierre Bourdieu, Ann Swidler, Michael Shudson, Robert Wuthnow, and Steve Durné—on the question of motivation, to see what they say.

Human Motivation in Cultural Theory

Pierre Bourdieu

The late Bourdieu was a world-class giant in the field of cultural sociology whose mark is evident in the widespread use of his ideas of "fields" of struggle, "habitus," cultural capital, social practices, symbolic violence, distinction, and the "misrecognition" of power relations. On first reading, Bourdieu seems to grant culture's symbolic sphere of meaning a crucially influential place in his analysis. He explicitly rejects both rational choice's *Homo economicus* view of human action and the traditional Marxist superstructure/infrastructure distinction, claiming instead that symbols and culture play a critical role in the production and maintenance of social life. Bourdieu claims to offer a nonreductionistic account of cultural life. His own substantive work involves studies of art worlds,

3. Colin Campbell makes a similar point with reference to British sociology in his *The Myth of Social Action* (Cambridge: Cambridge University Press, 1996).

consumption patterns, Algerian peasant culture, educational practices, cultural tastes and styles, and intellectual production. With Bourdieu, it appears that culture is given a place of prominence by a scholar of major importance.[4]

But Bourdieu's interest in symbols and meaning turns out to take on a different shade of importance when understood in light of his view of human motivation. At bottom, Bourdieu is a thoroughgoing materialist who believes that practical activity is the underlying unity of all of social life; and that the fundamental human motive is the self-interested accumulation of power and status. This is not for Bourdieu a hypothesis seeking empirical validation but an axiomatic presupposition that determines all in his thought that follows.[5] With Bourdieu, culture turns out to operate always within a political economy that is invariably reward seeking, and human action is expressed in strategies concerned with the "maximizing of material and symbolic profit."[6] Thus Bourdieu sees his task as constructing "a general theory of the economy of practices"[7] that is "capable of treating all practices, including those that are experienced as disinterested or gratuitous, and therefore freed from the 'economy,' as economic practices aimed at maximizing material and symbolic profit."[8] Elsewhere he writes similarly that we should "abandon the dichotomy of the economic and the non-economic which stands in the way of seeing the science of economic practices as a particular case of a general science of the economy of practices, capable of treating all practices, including those purporting to be disinterested or gratuitous, and hence non-

---

4. Bourdieu's publications are voluminous, but, for starters, see Pierre Bourdieu, *Outline of a Theory of Practice* (Cambridge: Cambridge University Press, 1977); *Distinction: A Social Critique of the Judgement of Taste* (Cambridge: Harvard University Press, 1984); *The Logic of Practice* (Stanford, Calif.: Stanford University Press, 1990); *In Other Words: Essays toward a Reflexive Sociology* (Stanford, Calif.: Stanford University Press, 1990); *The Field of Cultural Production* (New York: Columbia University Press, 1993).

5. David Swartz, *Culture and Power: The Sociology of Pierre Bourdieu* (Chicago: University of Chicago Press, 1997).

6. Bourdieu, *The Logic of Practice*, 16.

7. Bourdieu, *Outline of a Theory of Practice*, 177.

8. Bourdieu, *The Logic of Practice*, 122.

economic, as economic practices directed toward the maximizing of material or symbolic profit."[9]

But what is symbolic profit? Perhaps something derived from other than material interests? No, says Bourdieu, for "economic capital is at the root of all other types of capital," including cultural and symbolic capital, which are in the end merely "transformed, disguised forms of economic capital."[10] Again, elsewhere Bourdieu writes that "symbolic capital, a transformed and thereby disguised form of physical 'economic' capital . . . originates in 'material' forms of capital which are also, in the last analysis, the source of its effects."[11] Thus Bourdieu appears to make no Weberian distinction between "instrumentally rational" and "value rational" action. Rather, Caillé appears to be correct in saying that his theory is one of "economic determination in the last instance."[12] Even the sympathetic Craig Calhoun suggests that

> the motive force of social life [for Bourdieu] is the pursuit of distinction, profit, power, wealth, and so on. Bourdieu's account of capital is an account of the resources people use in such pursuit. In this sense, despite his disclaimers, Bourdieu does indeed share a good deal with Gary Becker and other rational choice theorists. . . . He accepts the notion of interest, albeit as part of a "deliberate and provisional reductionism" in order to be able to show that cultural activity is not "disinterested." . . . [T]hough Bourdieu points out the historical particularity of all interests, he does not deny the universality of interested action. Implicitly, at least, he goes further, beyond treating all action simply as interested—which is little more than saying "motivated." He treats all interests . . . as formally simi-

9. Bourdieu, *Outline of a Theory of Practice*, 183.

10. Pierre Bourdieu, "The Forms of Capital," in J. G. Richardson (ed.), *Handbook of Theory and Research for the Sociology of Education* (New York: Greenwood, 1986), 252.

11. Bourdieu, *Outline of a Theory of Practice*, 183.

12. Caillé is quoted in Swartz, *Culture and Power*, 68; the subordinate and dominated quotes below come from Swartz, *Culture and Power*, 79. Not all theorists, however, are entirely persuaded by this interpretation; see, for example, Bourdieu's own "A Reply to Some Objections," in Bourdieu, *In Other Words*, 106–19. Also see chapters in Craig Calhoun, Edward LiPuma, and Moishe Postone (eds.), *Bourdieu: Critical Perspectives* (Chicago: University of Chicago Press, 1993).

lar in their implication of strategies designed to advance some manner of acquisition of power or wealth. Bourdieu is saying something more trans-historical and anthropologically invariant about human actors than he lets on.[13]

Culture, therefore, for Bourdieu, turns out finally not to be a strong source of human value, direction, purpose, or motivation itself. Rather, culture is a tool or resource, certainly operating on its own field of production and struggle but ultimately at the service of material interests. It may serve this purpose consciously or unconsciously, directly or indirectly. But the pursuit of power and material gain are what culture is ultimately about, since cultural capital is subordinate to and dominated by economic capital.[14] Thus, although most aspects of Bourdieu's theoretical approach depart significantly from rational choice theory, when it comes to the specific question of human *motivation for action*, Bourdieu's approach appears at bottom not entirely different from the view of motives postulated by rational choice theory—even if symbols play a much more important role in the pursuit of its ends.

Bourdieu's approach to the study of religion, for example, which is laid out in his essay "Genesis and Structure of the Religious Field," is instructive in this regard.[15] Synthesizing Marx and Durkheim, Bourdieu presents a functionalist view of religion as always deriving from and reproducing the political and material interests of dominant social classes. The sociological task thus is to analyze "the political functions that religion fulfills for various social classes in a given social formation by virtue of its strictly symbolic efficacy." According to Bourdieu, given the Marxist concern with social class division and Durkheim's insight about the social origins of consciousness,

> one is necessarily driven to the hypothesis that a correspondence exists between social structures (strictly speaking, power structures) and mental

13. Craig Calhoun, "Habitus, Field, and Capital," in Calhoun et al., *Bourdieu*, 70–71.

14. Swartz, *Culture and Power*, 79.

15. Pierre Bourdieu, "Genesis and Structure of the Religious Field," in Craig Calhoun (ed.), *Comparative Social Research, A Research Annual, Religious Institutions* (Greenwich, Conn.: JAI Press, 1991); the following two quotes come, respectively, from pp. 5, 17–18.

structures. This correspondence obtains through the structure of symbolic systems, language, religion, art, and so forth; or, more precisely, religion contributes to the (hidden) imposition of the principles of structuration of the perception and thinking of the [social] world ... insofar as it imposes a system of practices and representations whose structure, objectively founded on a principle of political division, presents itself as the natural-supernatural structure of the cosmos.

For Bourdieu, it is the material conditions of existence that determine life and consciousness; religion is the derivative object of the material world's influence:

> Religious interest is based on the need to legitimate the material or symbolic properties attached to a determinate type of conditions of existence and position in the social structure and, consequently, it depends directly on this position. Thus, the religious message most capable of satisfying the religious interest of a determinate group of laypeople ... is that which carries a (quasi) system of justification of the properties that are objectively attached to it as it occupies a determinate position in the social structure.

Religion thus always serves the ideological function of legitimating through reinforcement the objective structures of material inequality:

> Religion is predisposed to assume an ideological function, a practical and political function of absolutizing of the relative and legitimation of the arbitrary. It can fulfill this function ... by ... reinforcing the material or symbolic strength that can be mobilized by a group or class to legitimate all that which socially defines this group or class ... which [is] objectively attached to it inasmuch as it occupies a determining position in the social structure. ... Religion therefore adds the symbolic reinforcement of its sanctions to the limit and the ... barriers imposed by a determinant type of material conditions of existence.[16]

16. Bourdieu, "Genesis and Structure of the Religious Field," 14. And again: "The configuration of the structure of relations constitutive of the religious field ... fulfills an external function of legitimizing the established order inasmuch as the maintenance of the symbolic order contributes directly to the maintenance of the political order. ... An institution like the church, which finds itself invested with the function of maintaining the symbolic order by virtue of its position in the structure of the religious field, always contributes in addition to the maintenance of political order" (31, 33).

In sum, religion is not a semiautonomous cultural element with significant cognitive and moral capacity to employ narratives and normative commitments to form human consciousness and motivate human action *in any ways other than* in the pursuit of ultimately material interests. If religion for Bourdieu holds any capacity to be a source of human value, direction, purpose, or motivation, that capacity is always, through correspondence, tied to and governed by the interests and imperatives of the materially determinate structure of social and political relations. In other words, if and insofar as culture motivates people at all, those motives will finally be determined by reward-seeking practices directed toward the "maximizing of material or symbolic profit," which at bottom is economic profit. And on this particular point of motivation, I suggest, Bourdieu shares a great deal theoretically with rational choice theory.

Bourdieu has made tremendous contributions to our understanding of the workings of culture and power. His work as a whole is, of course, much more sophisticated and nuanced than this brief summary could convey. But when it comes specifically to the focused question of human *motivation* for action, Bourdieu provides a less than satisfying account for sociologists interested in a theory of culture as an explanatory source of human action not significantly derived from and governed by some "deeper" or "more fundamental" social reality—such as the structure of relations of economic inequality—and not merely at the service of material self-interest.

Ann Swidler

Swidler's influential 1986 article "Culture in Action" presents a similar problem.[17] In it she seeks to develop a theory of "cultural explanation," to understand how and why culture may exert an "independent causal role" in ways that "directly shape" human action. Swidler first claims that the old Weberian and Parsonian model is no longer credible. Human

---

17. Ann Swidler, "Culture in Action: Symbols and Strategies," *American Sociological Review* 51 (1986): 273–86; quotes in the following three paragraphs come from pp. 283, 273, 276, 277, 279, 284. My critique here is similar to that of Craig Calhoun, "Introduction: Social Issues in the Study of Culture," *Comparative Social Research* 11 (1989): 15–16.

action is clearly not determined by internalized interests and values that are determined by culture and that specify for actors the proper ends of action. "Culture," she writes, "does not influence how groups organize action via enduring psychological proclivities implanted in individuals by their socialization." Instead, Swidler advances a view of culture as a "toolkit" of symbolic vehicles (stories, rituals, worldviews, etc.) that people use "to solve different kinds of problems." Culture thus determines the pattern of symbolic components people have available with which to construct "strategies of action"—by which she means "ways of trying to organizing a life . . . within which particular choices make sense, and for which particular, culturally shaped skills and habits . . . are useful." Strategies of action in turn allow actors to pursue "different life goals." What matters causally about culture, then, is its influence on the shape and organization of the links in chains of action, not in determining the ends of action.

Many of Swidler's criticisms of older theories of culture are well taken. She is correct in observing that "people do not choose their actions one at a time" and that "people construct chains of action beginning with at least some pre-existing links." Swidler is also right in arguing that "a culture is not a unified system that pushes action in a consistent direction" and that culture does not provide "the underlying assumptions of an entire way of life." Also true enough, culture is not "some free-floating heritage of ideas, myths, or symbols." And Swidler may also be correct in claiming that "styles or strategies of action [are] more persistent than the ends people seek to attain." Yet none of these observations necessarily precludes culture from providing people with normative ends that help to shape their action. In principle, all of these critiques may be valid, and culture may still help to provide actors the ends of action. Thus the persuasiveness of Swidler's argument hinges in part on identifying the idea of culture providing ends of action with the ideas of cultural unity and consistency; of original, individual choice; and of the persistence of ends to match the actions they historically generated. But it is not clear that either Weber or Parsons themselves equated all of these ideas.

More problematically, having dismissed the idea that culture shapes the ends of action as a view that has been "thoroughly criticized" and that sociologists do not "really believe in" any more, the question of ends nevertheless remains. Grant that culture is a toolkit that shapes strategies of action that help people solve problems, reach life goals, and make their choices make sense. We still need to ask: What determines what people think are problems that need solving? What determines what life goals one should try to reach? What determines the felt need to make a choice that may or may not make sense? If the answer is "strategies of action," then Swidler has merely taken the long route to arguing that culture determines the ends of action. But that is precisely the view she is criticizing. The answer could alternatively be that perceived problems, life goals, and the necessity of choices are distributed randomly or unpredictably and that the sociologist should ignore these questions and focus only on the shape of the strategies of action that influence their answers. But that hardly seems plausible, or very sociological.

A third possibility could be an implicit default into the rational choice assumption, that the supposedly universally "practical" matter of self-interestedly maximizing material rewards and benefits is what determines the problems people need to solve, the goals they seek to achieve, the choices they confront. If so, then culture has nothing to do with motivating human action. Material self-interest does. Rather, culture merely conditions the means that people use to pursue their material self-interest. In fact, in her article Swidler explicitly criticizes the rational choice model; but notably it is rational choice's individualism and teleology that Swidler critiques, not its theory of human motivation. Swidler also acknowledges that her approach "may seem at first to relegate culture to a subordinate, purely instrumental role in social life." But her retort that "strategies of action are cultural products" is not entirely satisfying; for within her own framework, it does not answer the lingering questions about ends, goals, problems, and decisions raised above. And Swidler's elaboration of this retort—that cultural elements "create moods and motivations, ways of organizing experience and evaluating reality, modes of regulating conduct, and ways of forming social bonds, which provide resources for constructing strategies of action"—itself only raises more questions. Motivations to do what, and why? Which experiences are people having, and why? Evaluating reality according to what scheme of values and purposes? Conduct enacted with what intention? One way or another, it appears that Swidler must or has smuggled in some theory about the determinates of the ends of human action, whether cultural or noncultural—and therefore about human motivation—without which her very helpful discussion about "toolkits," strategies of action, and settled versus unsettled lives lacks coherence.

Michael Shudson

Shudson has also taken up the question of how culture works in a 1989 article titled just that: "How Culture Works."[18] In setting up his own argument, Shudson offers a critique of Swidler similar to that suggested above, venturing that her position "assigns culture no efficacy in social action at all. It suggests that while people may need a symbolic object to define, explain, or galvanize a course of action [that] they have already decided on, an appropriate object will always be found to clothe the pre-existing intention." Shudson hopes to offer a more satisfying explanation for the influence of culture on human consciousness and action. He claims to want to explain why "sometimes culture 'works' and sometimes it doesn't" and "what determines whether cultural objects will light a fire or not." Shudson proceeds then to explicate quite nicely "the conditions . . . that are likely to make the culture or cultural object work more or less [well]." These, he suggests, include what he labels retrievability, rhetorical force, resonance, institutional retention, and resolution—the meanings of which I need not explain here. Suffice it to say that the more of each of these factors is present in any situation, the more effectively culture works.

Shudson's argument is smart, clear, and persuasive. The only problem is that it does not answer his own question of "how culture works." Nor does it elucidate what Swidler failed to explain: culture's efficacy in generating and directing social action. Instead—*simply assuming the (unexplained) fact that culture does "work" in some way or other*—Shudson merely identifies the variables that influence whether culture works more or less well in any situation. It is a perfectly legitimate, interesting, and constructive analysis that tells us *when* or *under what conditions* culture works. But since an underlying model of human motivations for action is unspecified, it brings us no closer to understanding more essentially *how* and *why* culture works than did Swidler.

18. Michael Shudson, "How Culture Works," *Theory and Society* 18 (1989); the following quotes come from pp. 156, 158, 160.

Robert Wuthnow

The work of Wuthnow in the theory of culture—particularly his book *Meaning and Moral Order*[19]—makes an interesting case for comparison, for he is quite deliberate in avoiding any focus on human motivation. According to Wuthnow, cultural approaches concerned with understanding the "ideas, moods, motivations, and goals" that are "internalized as part of the individual's worldview" involve "problems of evidence, method, and interpretation that would be desirable to avoid if possible." Wuthnow instead proposes to take his readers "beyond the problem of meaning," with its difficulties interpreting "radically subjective beliefs, attitudes, and meanings." Of scholarly interests in learning about the meanings of events in which people participate Wuthnow asks, "Is not this a hopeless task?" "More can be learned about the conditions under which a statement or act is meaningful," he writes, "than we can about its actual meaning."[20] More promising alternative methods for studying culture are what Wuthnow calls the structural, dramaturgical, and institutional approaches. These investigate not the meanings and values that motivate human action but instead, respectively, the internal boundaries, relations, and rules that structure objective symbolic objects; the capacity of rituals, ideologies, and other symbolic acts to dramatize the normative nature of social relations; and the deployment of institutional resources to ritualize, codify, and transmit cultural products.

Following this approach, Wuthnow's impressive tome *Communities of Discourse*[21] models a cultural analysis that pays primary "attention to the environmental resources used in ideological production, to the ways in which the producers of ideology and these resources come to be organized, and to the ways in which the ideology itself is internally structured"—and ignores "meanings and motivations [that are] nearly impos-

19. Robert Wuthnow, *Meaning and Moral Order* (Berkeley: University of California Press, 1987); quotes in this paragraph come from pp. 11, 60, 63, 65.

20. Already here one might ask how we can discern the conditions that make a statement or act meaningful unless we are able to determine meaningfulness itself; and, if we are able to do that, then why we cannot investigate "actual meaning"? Can such an analysis really ever escape the problem of human subjectivity?

21. Robert Wuthnow, *Communities of Discourse* (Cambridge: Harvard University Press, 1989); quotes are from pp. 17, 528.

sible to reconstruct." The absence of an account of human motivation for action in Wuthnow, then, is intentional and explicitly justified. And his analyses are tremendously rich, stimulating, and insightful.

Still, one wonders if Wuthnow has or ever really can leave behind subjective human motivation. One suspects that the approach he offers inevitably presumes some model of human personhood involving motives and purposes for it to make sense on its own terms. In the course of his argument, for example, Wuthnow defines ideology as "a set of symbols that articulates how social relations should be arranged" and culture as a "symbolic-expressive dimension of social structure [that] communicates information about morally binding obligations."[22] "Social life," he also observes, "requires a dimension of moral order, that is, a set of definitions about what is proper to do and what is reasonable to expect." But why, we might wonder, are the "shoulds" of morally binding obligations, moral order, and definitions of social obligations pervasive and crucial to human life? And what might that assume or suggest about human persons and motivation? Wuthnow further observes that the internal patterns of symbolic elements "give culture coherence and identity." But why does it matter that culture has coherence and identity for its human producers and users, and what might that tell us about these cultural animals? Elsewhere Wuthnow discusses the matter of human commitment, noting that "whether a person is 'committed to' an idea or belief is . . . important because it reveals something about how one is likely to think and behave." Still, Wuthnow steers the reader "to think of commitment not primarily as a subjective state or inward predisposition, nor as 'the meaning' of a cultural element, but as a relatively discreet and observable relation between a symbolic statement and the person"—such as the use of a cultural repertoire of utterances and actions to express "sincerity" of conviction. This may be a useful analytical move. But one may still ask, what exactly is generating human expressions of sincere commitment? Why do people apparently become sincerely committed to ideas and beliefs? Why and how do commitments affect people's thoughts and behaviors? And, again, what might all this suggest about the kind of animals that humans are?

This line of questioning can continue. In *Communities of Discourse*, Wuthnow discusses what historical actors such as Luther, Voltaire, and

22. Wuthnow, *Meaning and Moral Order*, 12, 13, 14, 338.

Marx were able to accomplish in producing innovative ideologies.[23] He notes the high levels of "popular demand for reform" in the cities of central Europe in the sixteenth century and that Protestant Reformers were able to engage in "creative acts" in their work. Wuthnow refers to the visions and symbolic frameworks that the Reformers offered their followers, which provided the cultural resources needed "for the individual to function as a morally responsible actor," as well as ideologies as "moral constructs that specified models for behavior." He suggests the analytical value of the concept of "social horizons" for understanding ideological change—by which he means "the real, experienced social context in which ideology is produced, selected, and institutionalized." Wuthnow also claims that the intellectual conflicts generated in key times of social change are not reducible to economic or political forces but also significantly involve things like "different views of the Eucharist" (in the Reformation) and "strong personalities" (in the Enlightenment). Summing up his entire argument, Wuthnow says that history is not only shaped by political and economic interests and conditions but "is made by actors who exercise choice on the basis of partial information."[24]

But again I ask: Why do actors even act? What motivates them to pursue one thing instead of another, or anything at all? What, if it is more than external conditions only, propels human action, which is then shaped by external conditions? Wuthnow has made great gains in focusing not on the motives for but on the social conditions—"environmental conditions," "institutional contexts," "discursive fields," and so on—that shape historic ideological change. But can such an analysis finally ignore the question of human motivation? Wuthnow must at least implicitly rely on some idea about why Luther, Voltaire, and Marx wanted to accomplish their work, why citizens of cities would demand reform, why the Reformers were motivated to act creatively. He must hold some assumptions

---

23. Wuthnow, *Communities of Discourse*, 12, 15, 17, 119, 130, 149–50, 557, 564, 582.

24. Morawska and Spohn rightly note, however, that, "while Wuthnow's theoretical model . . . requires . . . producers engaged in action sequences, there is actually little human activity in his historical analysis" (" 'Cultural Pluralism' in *Historical Sociology*," 59). Also see Calhoun, "Introduction: Social Issues in the Study of Culture," 16–17.

about human personhood in emphasizing the importance of people functioning as "morally responsible actors" and moral constructs that specify models of behavior. There must be something of importance in human subjectivity behind Wuthnow's claim that "real, experienced" social horizons influence historical actors, who are driven in part by personality types and beliefs about religious rituals. The point is not that Wuthnow himself should have necessarily elaborated a theory of human personhood and motivation. His work in culture has already contributed more than anyone could ask or expect. The point, rather, is simply that Wuthnow, like the others examined above, does not elaborate such a theory—even if, arguably, his analysis, like all analyses, ultimately must presume one theory or another.

Steve Durné

Finally, I examine a chapter by Steve Durné—"Cultural Conceptions of Human Motivation and Their Significance for Cultural Theory," published in Diana Crane's 1994 book *The Sociology of Culture: Emerging Theoretical Perspectives*[25]—because its focus on human motivation directly addresses the central concern of this chapter. Durné begins by observing that "despite its recent resurgence, culture theory has failed to develop a convincing model of culture's causal effects." He notes that the Weberian-Parsonian model of culture (as supplying actors with ends and values) has been rejected for good reasons: because people contest the norms of their culture and interpret cultural symbols in diverse ways, and because different kinds of action can arise among people who share the same values. But, Durné notes, this "leaves scholars with a theoretical dilemma. . . . The rejection of the idea of shared cultural values has proved difficult to reconcile with the idea that culture 'exert[s] some regular influence on the behavior of group members.' "[26] Quite so. In response, Durné sets out in this chapter to offer an account of culture's causal effects on human

---

25. Crane, *The Sociology of Culture*. Durné quotes in the following text come from pp. 267, 268, 272, 274, 275, 276, 282, 285.

26. Durné here is quoting Peter Stromberg, "Consensus and Variation in the Interpretation of Religious Symbols," *American Ethnologist* 8 (1981): 545.

action that is consistent with the fact that people do not always share social norms and that they often "buck [the] social norms" they do share.

Durné then makes a crucial move. He shifts the locus of explanation away from human motivation and instead to culture's capacity only externally to *restrain* action. He writes, "I shift the focus from prescriptive elements of culture like values, to commonsense, but nonetheless cultural, descriptions people use to orient themselves to the world." These informal, commonsense cultural understandings of human motivation—what he calls "social frameworks for understanding action"—have the causal effect of limiting or constraining the (Swidlerian) "strategies of action" people use to negotiate life. According to Durné, they do this "by determining the picture individuals need to present [of] themselves to avoid being distrusted as someone whose actions make no sense." Thus cultural "understandings constrain . . . not by actually shaping motivations. Rather, understandings of motivation constrain individuals by driving social practices that attach real social consequences to the appearance of being motivated" by what are widely considered legitimate versus illegitimate motivations. In short, people do not want to suffer the costs of being defined as deviant, so they conform their explanations of the motivations for their actions to culturally dominant accounts of legitimate action, in order to be seen as normal and acceptable.

Note that Durné ignores the question of what over the long run determines what collectivities of people widely believe is legitimate, of why ultimately for people certain "actions make no sense" while other actions do; on this point he only mentions twice that cultural practices are determined by "powerful groups," whose self-interests those practices presumably serve (which leads us back to Bourdieu).

Thus we see that "commonsense understandings of what motivates people" do not reflect what actually motivates them. Rather they only "generate a vocabulary of legitimate action which constrains the strategies that individuals and social groups can use to pursue their own interests." But, we should ask, what then determines people's interests, if not culture? Durné does not say—though the answer is not hard to surmise. For the underlying model of human personhood and action that emerges here looks like that of rational choice theory: humans act in the context of opportunity and constraint to pursue their self-determined, self-oriented, material interests. Durné's twist is simply in adding culture to the list of external structures that constrain action. In this light, culture is conceptualized as something entirely external to people: culture "defin[es] the social understandings that actors must contend with" and shapes the social practices that "individuals confront as external constraints." Furthermore, "individual desires" are, if anything, oriented toward "breaking with social norms." Thus people not only resist culture but also work to *exploit* it as best they can to their own advantage. According to Durné, they strategically engage in "culture work"—"the combination and manipulation of cultural components . . . to attribute meaning to particular actions"—in order "to avoid the discredit of appearing to lack what are defined as normal human attributes." Similarly, he writes, people use culture "to justify their actions" and "deliberately mimic" cultural conventions "to conceal their unacceptable agendas."

In effect, what at first appears to be an account of human motivation from the perspective of the theory of culture turns out to be an interpretation of the ways human actors as "culture users . . . manipulate cultural symbols for their own purposes." People are not informed by culture to negotiate life. Rather, they are informed by . . . what? An *unspecified something*—perhaps material self-interest?—to "negotiate . . . elements of the cultural apparatus." Culture, in other words, is not something that constitutes, motivates, empowers, and guides people and their actions. It is only something that people *use* to achieve purposes that are presumably not specified by culture. This difficulty is not Durné's alone but, I am suggesting in this chapter, a common problem in much of contemporary cultural sociology.

Again, much in Durné's chapter is interesting and insightful. But absent from it is any explanation of human motivation that takes culture seriously. Durné writes that people engage in "tactics . . . to pursue diverse, but particular goals." But how do people know among the many potential goals which goals to pursue and which not, if not through their culture? Durné writes that people both are constrained by and manipulate cultural accounts of their actions in order to be seen by others as normal. But what is it that determines and over time sustains shared standards of "normal"? And why over the long run would those others for whom actors perform—who themselves are also interested, strategic actors—hold an individual actor to demanding standards of "normal" and "legitimate"?

Why would they do this if they did not actually internally believe in the standards themselves—that is, if they did not function as some kind of internalized cultural norms? Instead of expending the costs to punish abnormal and illegitimate actors, why not simply together revise the standards of "normal" to make life easier for all? Or, to use a different image, would not the inmates in a prison of which they were also simultaneously the only guards eventually simply set themselves free, unless they somehow truly believed in the importance and legitimacy of the prison itself?[27] Durné set out to explain culture's "causal effect" on human action. In fact, he has only explained culture's *conditioning* effect. Culture in Durné does not motivate human action. And what exactly does remains unexplained.

Conclusion

The contemporary literature in the sociology of culture—including but going well beyond the works considered above—can leave one with an odd feeling. Cultural sociology has been resurgent in the last twenty years precisely in order to provide much richer cultural accounts of human social life and action than the "structuralist," neo-Marxist, and rational choice theories of the 1970s and 1980s did. But much in recent cultural theory in sociology actually seems to be grounded on essentially rational choice assumptions about human motives and action. And other works in culture that are not seem reluctant or unable to offer accounts of human action that fit and justify their own theoretical and empirical arguments. One reads the literature to try to discover a renewed and deepened appreciation and understanding of the influence of culture in human social life, a thickly culturalist account of the patterns of social action and relations. But instead what one often finds are approaches in which culture does not explain action, or assumptions about human motivations and action that are not shaped by culture, or simply nothing said about human motives, purposes, or actions at all.[28]

27. This image is borrowed from Peter Berger's *Invitation to Sociology* (New York: Anchor Doubleday, 1963), 120–21.

28. This observation, however, is not to underestimate more general interest and strategies within and around sociology over time to bring a stronger sense of

This is no doubt partly a result of some of the specific directions that studies in culture have taken in the last two decades, directions that have themselves helped to revive today's interest in culture. In the "old days," culture used to focus on goals, consensus, unity, consistency, and integration—all of which fit nicely, if misguidedly, a concern with patterns of human belief and motivation. Today the emphasis in culture is on difference, contradiction, incongruence, domination, and resistance—most of which comport with rational choice theory's anthropological premises.

The lack of robust accounts of human action and motivation in culture theory is also surely the result of broader and related intellectual trends in the academy that more generally undermine the project of understanding human motivation, intentions, and action. We have learned, for example, to doubt our capacity to discover "authorial intent," to question whether human words can convey any intended meaning other than those constructed by their hearers and readers for themselves. We read that human subjects do not actually make history but are, rather, entirely constituted and driven by world-historical "epistemes" and "regimes of truth." We have been told that humanity holds nothing in common worth speaking of, that there is only relativity and "difference all the way down." We have learned to read "texts" not to discover the visions and beliefs and arguments they contain but rather to deconstruct them into the infinite number of possible interpretive readings they might sustain. We are then assured that all human behavior and institutions are only the result of "genes" that have been "selected on" for their success in "reproductive fitness" in the process of human evolution. These kind of intellectual precepts, now ubiquitous in the humanities and influential in the social sciences, make trying to think seriously about motivated human action

---

the acting person into theory and explanation, including, for a few examples: Mary Douglas, *Missing Persons: A Critique of the Social Sciences* (Berkeley: University of California Press, 1998); Campbell, *The Myth of Social Action;* Raymond Boudon, *The Logic of Social Action* (London: Routledge and Kegan Paul, 1979); Dennis Wrong, "The Oversocialized Conception of Man in Modern Sociology," *American Sociological Review* 26 (1961): 183–93; Herbert Blumer, *Symbolic Interaction* (Englewood Cliffs, N.J.: Prentice-Hall, 1969). Also see Robert Paul, "What Does Anybody Want?: Desire, Purpose, and the Acting Subject in the Study of Culture," *Cultural Anthropology* 5, no. 4 (1990): 431–51.

seem rather quaint, if not pitifully misguided. So much the worse for us intellectually.

Of course there is plenty of interesting and insightful work to be done in culture that is not focused on motivation and action—including studies of patterned relations within and among symbol systems themselves; analyses of political and economic conditions shaping the production, diffusion, reception, and institutionalization of cultural objects; investigations into the role of symbolic elements in processes of social reproduction and oppression; and much more. However, *I suggest that it is impossible for a cultural sociology worth pursuing to avoid entirely articulating a model of human personhood, motivation, and action in decidedly cultural terms.*[29] If we do not, one alternative model will rush in to fill the vacuum: the clearly articulated (though erroneous) model of rational choice theory. And it appears that it already has, to some degree. But if we relinquish to rational choice the theorizing of human personhood, we have effectively marginalized culture into relative insignificance. Culture then necessarily becomes simply one among many "tactics" or "constraints" or "tools" that will in the final analysis play second or third fiddle to political and economic factors considered to be more real or important or influential than symbols, meanings, narratives, and discourse.

We may choose to avoid discussions of human personhood, motivation, and action because they smack of passé debates about "human nature." But every analysis of human social life finally does rely, implicitly if not explicitly, on some model of human motivation for action. And if we are not willing or able to articulate a culture-centered model, then we will most likely default into the available alternative: rational choice's rational egoism—which hardly represents a "cultural turn" worth following. An alternative I suggest we consider is the moral, believing, narrating animals approach developed in these pages.

29. Again, for a parallel argument, see Campbell, *The Myth of Social Action.*

SEVEN

CONCLUSION

This book is written out of dissatisfaction with current influential theoretical systems purporting to explain human action and social life powerfully and comprehensively. Included among these are rational choice theory, exchange theory, sociobiology, evolutionary psychology, and associated approaches rooted in the naturalistic, utilitarian, antimentalist, noncultural tradition of Western social theory. I have sought in these pages to explicate some of the intellectual defects I see in these theories and to suggest an alternative approach that I believe more successfully handles many of these problems. In so doing, I have not only narrated my own theoretical story. I have also renarrated these other theories' stories within the framework of my own, redefining their intellectual significance in terms of the larger moral and political project that my story suggests they are pursuing, which more than anything makes them so compelling to so many moral, believing scholars. I conclude here by summarizing key aspects of my argument and suggesting some final implications.

These pages have sought to address the question of the particular kind of animals human beings are, in hopes of improving and enlarging our understanding of human social action and institutions. This book has advanced one approach to answering this question, arguing that the most adequate approach to theorizing human culture and social life must be a normative one that conceives of humans as moral, believing, narrating animals and human social life as constituted by moral orders that define and direct social action. Human culture, I have suggested, is always moral order, and human cultures are everywhere moral orders. Human persons, I have claimed, are nearly inescapably moral agents, human actions necessarily morally constituted and propelled practices, and human institutions inevitably morally infused configurations of rules and resources. Building on this model, in the foregoing pages I have suggested that one of the central and fundamental motivations for human action is to act out and sustain moral order, which constitutes, directs, and makes significant human life itself. This book has argued that human persons nearly universally live in social worlds that are thickly webbed with moral assumptions, beliefs, commitments, and obligations. The relational ties that hold human lives together, the conversations that occupy people's mental lives, the routines and intentions that shape their actions, the institutions within which they live and work, the emotions they feel every day—I have suggested that all of these and more are drenched in, patterned by, glued together with moral premises, convictions, and obligations. There is thus nowhere a human can go to escape moral order, no way to be human except through moral order. And until we recognize this and build into our theories the recognition that to enact and sustain moral order is one of the central, fundamental motivations for human action, our understanding of human action and culture will be impoverished.

These pages have claimed an intimate connection between moral order and social institutions. The moral is not simply a subjective concern limited to religion, ethical rules, or personal values. Neither are institutions merely practical arrangements for accomplishing functional tasks. Morally constituted and permeated worlds exist "inside" of people, in their assumptions, expectations, beliefs, aspirations, thoughts, judgments, and feelings. But they also exist outside of people, in structured social practices and relationships within which people's lives are embedded. Thus, social institutions are always morally animated enterprises, embedded within and giving expression to moral orders that generate, define, and govern them. Whether apparent or not, social institutions are inevitably rooted in and expressions of the narratives, traditions, and worldviews of moral orders. This means that the moral order that motivates and shapes human action is not merely something internalized through socialization—human action is not simply the external behavioral product of individuals' internal programming, directives, or specified ends. Rather, moral order permeates all aspects of the social order within which human lives are embedded and from which human animals draw their identities and capacities. Moral order inundates human social existence. It pervades the structured configurations of resources and practices that comprise our organizations and institutions. Moral order is thus woven into and indeed defines the very woven patterns of the social fabric itself, positioning moral order as external to and objectively existent for human actors. At the same time, precisely because human actors are constituted, developed, propelled, and guided by the social institutions in which their lives are embedded, the moral orders that animate social institutions also find imperfectly corresponding expression *within* human actors—in the assumptions, ideas, values, beliefs, volitions, emotions, and so on of human subjectivity, conscience, consciousness, and self-consciousness. The humans that both produce and are produced by social institutions thus engage moral order both objectively and subjectively. And the moral orders both inside and outside of human persons reflect and reproduce each other. This duality is lived in practice through a unified process that is historical, dialectical, and reciprocally self-reinforcing.

This approach, I have claimed, helps us to avoid a number of besetting missteps in cultural theory. It enables us to speak of internally motivated, purposive human action, without stumbling into the oversimplifications inherent in the Parsonian view of culture as instilling in actors the ends of action. It justifies our taking a strong position on the power and importance of socialization in social reproduction, without conceiving of those socialized as passive recipients of cultural norms, values, and ends— since they are always both the objects and subjects of their own socialization. The approach here allows us to think about society as truly having an ordered cultural system, without supposing that such a system is unified, consensual, well bounded, and always integrating. This model also enables us to recognize and analyze the externally constraining influence of culture without losing sight of the simultaneous internally motivating dimension of culture. It conceives of culture in a way that allows it both to provide instrumental tools for accomplishing purposive ends and to define purposes of human action themselves in relation to the right, true, and good of a moral order or orders. This model also allows us to speak of the subconscious, unintentional, and institutional-practice aspects of culture's role in social reproduction, without losing the creative and purposive dimensions of reproduction and transformation. Finally, the model described in these pages provides an account for notions of human freedom and responsibility that does not lapse into liberal political theory's fictional notions of individual autonomy and self-determined moral agency.

This book's argument has also made related claims about our human epistemological condition, suggesting that, contrary to foundationalist and positivist dreams, at bottom we humans are all really believers. The lives that we live and the knowledge we possess are based crucially on sets of basic assumptions and beliefs that themselves cannot be empirically verified or established with certainty, that are not universal, and for which no "deeper," more objective or independent, common body of facts or knowledge exists to adjudicate between. We build up our lives from presuppositional starting points in which we (mostly unconsciously) place our trust and that are not derived from other justifying grounds. Thus what we know about life and the world, about how life ought to be lived, is not founded on an indubitable, universal foundation of knowledge. Rather, we are all inescapably trusting, believing animals, creatures that must and do place our faith in beliefs that cannot themselves be verified except by means established by the presumed beliefs themselves.

Understanding ourselves as not only moral but also believing animals suggests implications for sociological work. First, this helps account for the tremendous diversity of human cultures and practices. Since knowledge is not founded on one universal and indubitable foundation but is rather built up from sets of starting-point assumptions and beliefs that are often very different from each other, humans are in a situation of tremendous world-defining openness that leads to a diversity of cultural outcomes. Recognizing that we are at bottom believing animals also helps to explain our persistent practice of sacralizing physical and mental objects. Humans are never simply believers in purely practical, functional terms but are recurrently, almost impulsively, believers in systems of knowledge and practice that involve sacreds and profanes. We are moral animals, in part, because we are believing animals, and the character of our believing inevitably inclines toward sacralization, the differentiation of sacred from profane. Humans do not believe primarily in detached, abstract, practical modes. Our believings are what create the conditions and shape of our very perceptions, identity, agency, orientation, purpose— in short, our selves, our lives, and our worlds as we know them. Finally, recognizing that we humans are believers at our core means that we will never really understand human social life if we do not pay close attention to the content and function of the beliefs that humans together hold and build their lives on. We need to see, in other words, that the starting-point presuppositions, assumptions, beliefs, and commitments of human communities have important ramifications for the character of those communities' practices, perceptions, and institutions. Basic beliefs have consequences. This means that sociological research programs that are fundamentally naturalistic, utilitarian, antimentalist, or noncultural will inevitably fail to understand human persons, consciousness, actions, and institutions. They are projects very badly gauged to address their subject of study and so necessarily have ended and will end in frustration, if not dead-ended failure. Indeed, they are actually themselves, rightly understood, historically situated moral projects, built up from presuppositions and assumptions that cannot be independently verified and championed by devotees who (more or less consciously) believe in these projects' moral worth.

Human culture and motivation to action are not at bottom instrumentally functional or practically rational matters but rather are very much normative concerns. It is orientation to moral order, I have suggested, and not innate acquisitiveness or functional practicality that most powerfully moves and guides human action. And the substance of most of our most important beliefs and moral orders come from the narratives in which our lives are embedded. The human animal is a moral, believing animal—inescapably so. And the larger cultural frameworks within which the morally oriented believings of the human animal make sense are most deeply narrative in form. We are the makers, tellers, and believers of narrative construals of existence and history, every bit as much as our forebears at any other time in human history. Furthermore, we are not only animals who make stories but also animals who are made by our stories. We tell and retell narratives that themselves come fundamentally to constitute and direct our lives. We thus cannot live without stories, big stories finally, to tell us what is real and significant and to know who we are, where we are, what we are doing, and why. Narrative is our most elemental human genre of communication and meaning-making, an essential way of framing the order and purpose of reality. Most other forms of abstract, rational, analytical discourse are always rooted in, contextualized by, and significant because of the underlying stories that narrate our lives. Thus cultures and motivations are not random, arbitrary, inexplicable jumbles of categories and ideas, not even assorted collections of cultural tools in toolkits. Yet that is not because of the ordering power of some given "deep structure" but rather because culture and motivation are generated and sustained by various narrative constitutions of what for moral, believing animals is real, significant, and good. The normative is thus organized by the narrative.

People thus most fundamentally understand what reality is, who they are, and how they ought to live by locating themselves within the larger narratives that they hear and tell, which constitute what is real and significant for them. Yet people who are in fact under the influence of a narrative may not fully recognize all elements of its story in their own lives. That does not matter, does not reduce the power of the narrative in and over human life. It is not necessary for individuals to be fully aware of or articulate about the details or variants of the historical narratives that shape their lives, or to represent in their particular experience every element of the narrative story line. Most people relate to their narratives as actors swept up in the movement of grand historical drama. Their lives are embedded within and expressive of big stories, whether or not they can recognize every detail of any version of the story in their present life.

This book's argument has also suggested that every social order has the sacred at its core. Social orders are not merely populations carrying on instrumentally functional institutions but rather are ultimately held together and set into motion by particular ideas and ideals about themselves that comprise their collective identities, which give social orders their essential locations, orientations, and significance in the larger world. And the center of any collective identity is not instrumental functionality but believed-in ideals and images that are sacred—that are, for the social order, set apart, hallowed, protected, inviolable. Thus all social orders are in a sense ultimately religious, in the sense of having sacreds at heart, in the form of sacrosancts set apart from the ordinary and profane through and by which the social orders live, move, and have their being.

This book's chapter on religion extended some implications of the moral, believing, narrating animals approach to address the questions of religious persistence, secularization, religious influences in social life, the nature of religious belief and unbelief, and the question of religious origins. There I suggested that moral, believing animals are the kind of creatures about whom it is not odd to think that they would develop beliefs, symbols, and practices about the reality of a superempirical order that makes claims to organize and guide human life. Moral animals are inescapably interested in and guided by normative cultural orders that specify what is good, right, true, beautiful, worthy, noble, and just in life, and what is not. To be a human person requires locating one's life within a larger moral order by which to know who one is and how one ought to live. Human individuals and groups, therefore, must look beyond themselves for sources of moral order that are understood as not established by their own desires, decisions, or preferences but instead believed to exist apart from them, providing standards by which their desires, decisions, and preferences can themselves be judged. As believing animals, human faith in superempirical orders that make claims to organize and guide human life is not categorically different from the fundamental and continual acts of presupposing and believing in all of the other assumptions and ideas that make the living of life even possible. So humans being religious is epistemologically in continuity with the living of ordinary human life as a whole. Finally, as humans are narrating animals who experience life as lived through time, and who seek to make meaning of life and self through life-constituting and orienting narratives of many sorts, the superempirical orders of religion provide humans with compelling narratives linking cosmic, historical, and personal significance for individuals and communities across time. Thus the human condition and the character of religion quite naturally fit, cohere, complement, and reinforce each other.

All of this also suggests that to be nonreligious or secular does not mean that one is not a believer, that one does not continually place one's faith in premises, assumptions, and suppositions that cannot be objectively substantiated or justified without recourse to other believed-in premises, assumptions, and presuppositions. Everyone—the secularist and nonreligious included—is a believing animal, ultimately a person of faith. Furthermore, to be nonreligious or secular does not mean that one's life is not fundamentally organized and guided by a larger moral order above and beyond oneself. Everyone is a moral animal, is constituted, motivated, and governed by the moral orders existing inside and outside of themselves. All humans are really quite similar in most of these respects. Where they differ is in the particular cultural moral orders to which they commit their lives.

Finally, the previous chapter suggested that in recent sociological theorizing about culture something seems to be missing. Something that was lost in the rejection of structural functionalism—however problematic that approach was—remains lost, not only in the many uncultural theoretical approaches that followed in functionalism's wake but also in much recent sociological work in culture. What is missing, I have suggested, is a convincing account of human motivation. One reads the culture literature to try to discover a renewed and deepened appreciation and understanding of the influence of culture in human social life, a thickly culturalist account of the patterns of motivation in social action and relations. But much in contemporary cultural theory in sociology actually seems to be grounded on essentially rational choice assumptions about human motives and action. And other works in culture that are not seem reluctant or unable to offer accounts of human action that fit and justify their own theoretical and empirical arguments. Thus we find there approaches in which culture does not explain action, or assumptions about human motivations and action that are not shaped by culture, or simply nothing said about human motives, purposes, or actions at all. All of this, I have claimed, is inadequate. For it is impossible for a cultural sociology worth pursuing to avoid entirely articulating a model of human personhood, motivation, and action in decidedly cultural terms. The moral, believing, narrating animals view advanced in this essay, I suggest, offers an alternative approach to address this challenge.

What, then may be some broader implications of this view? First, it surely presents a problem for the Enlightenment ideas of foundationalist knowledge, universal reason, and the autonomously choosing individual. For human knowledge has no common, indubitable foundation. Human reason always and only operates in the context of particular moral orders that define and orient reason in particular directions. And human individuals hardly "enjoy" autonomy from the traditions, histories, and narratives that constitute and direct fundamental human identity and action.

Human life is simply far too dependent, interdependent, networked, constructed, and directed by the larger, cultural, moral orders that nurture, orient, and guide human motivations and actions for much of what the Enlightenment has taught us to be remotely plausible. Michael Sandel is quite right in observing that we humans are inevitably "encumbered," not autonomous, creatures.[1] This has profound implications not only theoretically for liberal political theory but practically for thinking, feeling, and acting in our daily lives. Being the kind of animals that we actually are, histories, beliefs, narratives, and traditions are not our enemies, at least not necessarily so. Seeing that we do not possess the option to escape belief and tradition into a realm of unfettered, "authentic," individual reason and choice, the crucial question then becomes: *which* rival beliefs, narratives, and traditions merit our allegiance and why? To submit ourselves to certain traditions—say, liberal individualism or market capitalism—on the premise that in so doing we are in fact escaping submission to tradition is self-deceiving. Certain beliefs, stories, and traditions can of course be destructive. But that does not make belief, story, and tradition per se destructive. In fact, they turn out to be the basis of our human identity and life. We are not only stuck with them. We can only thrive because of them.

But attacking Enlightenment modernism is not itself very new. Postmodernists have been doing that for years now. It would be wrong, however, to think that this essay's argument simply reiterates the postmodern story. For at least on one crucial point of this essay's story, many postmodernists falter as much as modernists do. That point again is individual autonomy. A typical postmodernist reaction against Enlightenment modernism has been to valorize the autonomous individual will engaged in unfettered self-creation and re-creation. Liberated from the constraints not only of tradition and moral order but also the dictates of universal reason, the individual self is set free to explore a fluid existence of eclectic self-definition, innovation, and metamorphosis with little need for a ra-

1. Michael Sandel, *Liberalism and the Limits of Justice* (Cambridge: Cambridge University Press, 1982); Michael Sandel (ed.), *Liberalism and Its Critics* (New York: New York University Press, 1984); also see Michael Sandel, *Democracy's Discontent: America in Search of a Public Philosophy* (Cambridge: Harvard University Press, 1996).

tionale or account. Self-identity derives from individual volition, little more. Thus ironically, for all of its attacks on Enlightenment modernism, contemporary postmodernism completely buys into the Enlightenment notion of the autonomous individual self. And this is not simply an intellectual affinity. It is a *shared moral commitment*. Although their differences tend to conceal that fact, the identity between them on this point is evident.

By contrast, this essay argues there is simply no humanness at all apart from moral order. Postmodernism wishes to liberate individuals from moral orders by granting the freedom of unfettered self-creation. Such a liberation is an illusion, a sociological absurdity. As heretical as it sounds to both modern and postmodern ears, it is necessarily only by giving ourselves to, indeed, by submitting ourselves to, specific moral orders derived from particular historical traditions that we can ever have anything like flourishing humanity.[2] The truly autonomous individual turns out to be a dead individual in every way imaginable.

Which brings us around to a last consideration of rational choice theory. It is not clear that the rational choice view of human persons as self-directed, self-interested material maximizers does not undermine its own emphasis on *choice* by proposing a single, monochromatic human motive—and by failing to provide a coherent account of the critical distance necessary to explain human creativity and innovation. When human choice revolves exclusively around calculated exchanges to maximize benefits, the substantive character of the choosing itself becomes thinner and thinner. Increasingly, the human chooser resembles a programmable calculator that simply inputs data, processes alternative scenarios, and outputs a decision based on relative values. When both the values of possible costs and benefits and the probabilities of realizing them are known, "choice" then essentially becomes a matter of crunching out numbers in a mathematical formula. The only wrinkle added is in having to predict the choices of other choosers that may affect the outcome of one's own

2. See Alasdair MacIntyre, *Three Rival Versions of Moral Enquiry: Encyclopedia, Genealogy, and Tradition* (Notre Dame, Ind.: University of Notre Dame Press, 1990); *After Virtue: A Study in Moral Theory* (Notre Dame, Ind.: University of Notre Dame Press, 1984); *Whose Justice? Which Rationality?* (Notre Dame, Ind.: University of Notre Dame Press, 1988).

choice—but even that, game theory has shown, can be calculated with enough iterations of the game.

In what sense, then, does human choice-making matter? Are not humans reduced to mere processors, perhaps even mere processes? Does not creativity come to mean simply the ability to adjust to new data? Is not agency merely another name for rationality, the ability to choose optimal ends for specified means? How, too, might the idea of human moral responsibility derive from this model? Or even morality itself? All that exist are relatively stable preferences that people seek to optimize. Could such a view of human persons ever produce a meaningful, robust political community? All that would seem to make sense would be a thin interest-group liberalism that itself merely calculates the costs and benefits of alternative divisions of the pie and chooses the optimal outcome. In all of this, the Western humanistic tradition emphasizing human rights, reflection, participation, responsibility, learning, deliberation, and community evaporates in the hum of calculations of costs and benefits. For that humanistic tradition only ultimately makes sense, I suggest, within a framework linking human choice and action to moral order.

Seeing the untenable implications of their theoretically clear but empirically flawed view of human personhood, the standard move of rational choice advocates has been to start to revise the assumptions of the model. Perhaps preferences are not stable but variable. Perhaps interests can be altruistic as well as selfish. Perhaps rewards can be ideal and material. Perhaps people do not maximize and optimize but merely "satisfice." Perhaps values and probabilities are typically not very well known. Et cetera. But this is a slippery slope that inevitably slides deeply into culture and morality. The revisionists are in the end no more truly rational choice analysts than are, say, "atheists" who have come sincerely and firmly to believe the Nicene Creed. The only shred that is left of rational choice is the idea that people generally do the things that they think they should do—which sounds a lot more like the descriptive anthropology of the moral, believing animals proposed in this book than anything resembling a rational choice theory worthy of attention. The slide into culture and morality is inexorable. For how now do we explain variability among "preferences?" Why would people seek "benefits" that are not selfish? Why is it that nonmaterial rewards compel action and choices? We reach a point where, for example, the modeling of Mother Teresa pouring out her life to live and work with the most diseased and wretched of humanity as a self-interested choice to maximize benefits ("given her particular preference structure"!) becomes grotesquely hilarious. The only way, once the slipping has started, to make sense of human social action is to take culture seriously by confronting human persons as moral, believing animals. At which point, we recover a notion of human choice worth having and using.

Having shifted to the moral, believing model of human personhood, we are able to see rational choice theory in a new and relativized light. It is not so much a scientific modeling of human behavior delivering quantitative precision and predictability but instead the abstract academic expression and promotion of the pervasive moral order animating market capitalism and political liberalism. It all comes together in a neat package that makes tremendous sense to the people so deeply socialized into that moral order. Rational choice thus proves to be as much a normative ideology as a scholarly analysis. Yet in the encounter of the two alternatives, the moral, believing model of human personhood is much more capable of solving the intellectual problems of rational choice and renarrating its significance within the terms and assumptions of its own intellectual tradition than vice versa. Which inevitably brings us back to the serious need to make sense of culture and morality.

Sociological theory cannot afford either to evade or to poorly answer questions of human personhood and motivation. We falter when we avoid them. And we are misled when we answer them in terms of the naturalistic, utilitarian, antimentalist, noncultural tradition of Western social theory. What we need instead is to face and embrace the fact that we human beings are moral, believing, narrating animals and to rethink our social theories and analyses in that light. Taking culture and morality seriously in this way, I suggest, will open up new and fruitful avenues of inquiry with significant implications for social research and for the living of life itself. Which of course is what scholarship is all about.

INDEX

abolitionists, American, 75
abortion, 51, 101
Adorno, Theodor, 86
agency, human agents, 20, 28–29, 31, 36, 47, 51n11, 55, 57, 148, 150–51
Alexander, Jeffrey, 127
Allah, 68
altruism, 34–36, 84; contrasted with morality, 14–15; reciprocal, 36
America, American, 18, 27, 67–68, 75, 88, 118
"American Experiment" narrative, 67, 69, 74–75, 78, 87
Amish, 103
Amnesty International, 102
angels, 99
Anglican church, 16
anthropology, 49, 79, 122, 127
anthropomorphizing, 107
antimentalism, antimentalist, 59, 147, 151, 158
antisocial personality disorder, 13
Arminianism, 27
artificial intelligence theory, 58
assumptions, presuppositions, 5, 8, 15, 38, 43n35, 46, 48–55, 57–61, 89–93, 100, 115, 119, 139, 143, 148–51, 153
atheism, 108, 111, 118, 122, 157

Augustine of Hippo, 55
authorial intent, 144
authority, 22
autobiographical narratives, 75
Ayala, Francisco, 39–40
Aztecs, 50

Bacon, Francis, 115n25
Baptist church, 77
Becker, Gary, 130
behaviorism, 58
beliefs, 7–10, 15, 27, 41–43, 46, 48–49, 51–55, 57–60, 79, 89, 96, 98, 119, 126, 137–38, 148–51, 153, 155; convictions, 15
Bell, Daniel, 127
Bellah, Robert, 77, 127
benefits. See rewards
Berger, Peter, 77, 109–11, 113
Bhaskar, Roy, 90
Bourdieu, Pierre, 127–33, 141
Brahma, 119
breaching experiments, 16
Buddhism, Buddha, 54, 96–97, 119
Bundy, Ted, 13

Calhoun, Craig, 81n13, 127, 130
Calvinism, 27